WITHDRAWN

The Struggle for Animal Rights

The Struggle for Animal Rights

TOM REGAN

International Society for Animal Rights, Inc.
Clarks Summit, PA

Published 1987

International Society for Animal Rights, Inc., and Culture
and Animals Foundation express gratitude to Claire and
Bill Allan for their support of this project.

Library of Congress Cataloging-in-Publication Data

Regan, Tom.
    The struggle for animal rights.

        1. Animals, Treatment of—United States.
        2. Animal experimentation—United States.   I. Title.
HV4764.R45   1987   179'.3'0973   87-80680
ISBN 0-9602632-1-7 (pbk.)

First printing 1987; Second printing 1988

To Helen Jones

who understood animal rights before the rest of us.

Contents

Preface

The essays collected here represent a fair sample of the informal writing I have been doing on the topic of animal rights during the past three years. Although each addresses a different topic, there is some overlap and even some repetition. I hope these latter points don't detract from the essays' interest or usefulness. If I were to attempt to edit them now, polishing them to a higher level of professional and literary sheen, I wouldn't have time to do other important things. Thus do they stand, on their own, as originally written and, in some cases, delivered.

These essays tell two stories. One is a story about me —about my struggle to find myself and, having done so, to make my life and work living instruments of social justice. The other is the story of the struggle for animal rights—or, to speak more precisely, a small part of that story, the part in which I have played some role. Each story is inseparable from the other. For I have reached that point in my life where it is no longer possible to talk about *who I am* without talking about *what I do*. And since what I mainly do is struggle for animal rights, the story of my life is the story of my involvement in that struggle. And vice versa. In the end, we are what we do.

One other thing I have come to recognize in these essays. Without having consciously set out to do so, I find that they paint a clear map of where the struggle for animal rights must be waged. There are battles to be fought in the classroom and the courts, in places of worship and before government bodies, in the marketplace and in the cafeteria line. These essays take the struggle for animal rights to these places and attempt to show the strength of the animal rights position, when properly understood. Others will add their efforts to mine, and many already have. Our Movement goes forward because of the work of many hands on many oars. Therein lies our strength.

That strength involves diversity, which is another way of describing the map these essays draw. We must reach out to all constituencies: to the religious community, the law, government, school administrators, the public at large. And we must learn to present our vision in new, bold ways and in new, unfamiliar places—in the theatre, for example, and in the concert hall, in factories and offices, before the blue bloods *and* the blue collars. If the Animal Rights Movement has suffered from anything, it's not been a failure of will. It's been a failure of imagination. My sincere hope is that these essays will help others imagine new possibilities. It's time we stopped serving the same old ideas in the same old ways. The animals for whom we struggle deserve better.

Tom Regan
Raleigh, NC
August 25, 1986

Introduction

by Colman McCarthy

My favorite passage in Russian literature is the monastery scene in "The Brothers Karamazov." Father Zossima, the compassionate and wise elder who has seen it all and survived it, is preaching a sermon to the community. One of the members is young Alyosha Karamazov. As a novice in the religious life, Alyosha is a dry well, ready to be filled with the waters of spiritual truth.

Father Zossima pours: "Brothers, have no fear of men's sin. Love a man even in his sin, for that is the semblance of Divine Love and is the highest love on earth. Love all God's creation, the whole and every grain of sand of it. Love every leaf, every ray of God's light. Love the animals, love the plants, love everything . . . Love animals; God has given them the rudiments of thought and joy untroubled. Do not trouble their joy, don't harass them, don't deprive them of their happiness, don't work against God's intent. Man, do not pride yourself on superiority to animals; they are without sin, and you, with your greatness, defile the earth by your appearance on it, and leave the traces of your foulness after you — alas, it is true of almost every one of us."

Few pieces of writing better stir our hearts to rethink our views on animals. But there is always the problem, once the stirring begins, how do you make other people — our families, our friends, our neighborhood and world — be good to animals? Obviously, you can't. The most that's possible, as Plato believed, is to work to create the conditions in which a person will want to be good.

Few others are creating these conditions with more passion, vision and intelligence than Tom Regan. Through his writing, teaching and activism — a rare trinity of excellence —he is helping to make a society in which all citizens can be good to animals because the moral conditions to exercise that goodness are easily available. "Good" is almost a meaningless word, so much so that it now has a pejorative context; some who get carried away with compassion, or other uncool exertions of the heart, are labeled "do-gooders." But when a philosopher like Tom Regan speaks of goodness we see the precision of its meaning. We are called, first, to decrease the amount of violence we inflict on animals and, second, to increase the breadth of justice we owe them. By being just to animals, we are being good to them. Justice is goodness.

The essays collected here are valuable for a number of reasons. First of all, the prose style flows with freshness. That alone is a cause for celebration. Philosophy may never be the same! Many philosophers give themselves dispensations from clarity, as if a grace with words will get them ejected from the faculty club.

Twinned with Tom Regan's prose gift is the also obvious one of scholarship. He has the masterly touch of the billiards player who sees three or four angles at once, where you and I see one. His multi-angled scholarship can be seen when he can as easily demolish the views of the 17th century's Descartes, who wrongly dismissed animals as "thoughtless brutes", as he can examine the violence behind rodeos or the Pentagon's wound labs. When this scholar is asked, "Where's the beef?" he answers that in the world of Wendy's and Big Macs the corpses of cows are "symptomatic of our culture's throwaway attitude toward animals, as if these sensitive creatures are commodities or things."

Each of these essays sparkles, but the deeper glow can be seen by those readers who savor connections. Professor Regan writes of his debt to Gandhi. The Hindu peacemaker, who honored animals with justice, often spoke of his gratitude to Tolstoy, with the Russian acknowledging his debt to Thoreau. In our own time, Martin Luther King, Jr., traveled to India to better study Gandhi, because Gandhi had been a devoted student of Christianity. To see Tom Regan joining this connected circle of philosophers and teachers is to understand, still again, that a fund of goodness and wisdom exists. It is a vast fund, to be tapped by all those who are trying to keep the faith and share the peace.

Since first writing about animal rights and human

wrongs in the 1960's, I have seen a circle widening. The courts, legislatures, schools, churches, media, and our own hearts, are now involved in ways undreamed of only 20 years ago. Much credit must go to Tom Regan. His careful thinking, expressed in these and many other essays, shows that the animal rights movement is grounded in morality. The strength of these essays is that they show a writer being a moralist but not a moralizer. He echos Father Zossima's call — "Love animals" — and then issues his own suggestions on how we might try to express that love. Each of us is called to our own expression. The beauty of these essays is that those novices who are just beginning — the Alyoshas — will find as much inspiration in Tom Regan's thoughts as those who are well along will find strength to go further. All of us, as Tom Regan is saying, are on safe ground because we are on moral ground.

The Struggle for Animal Rights

1

The Bird in the Cage:
A Glimpse of My Life

In the Fall of 1985, John Stockwell, the editor of *Between the Species,* approached me about contributing to the series of autobiographies featured in his important magazine. Even though the invitation carried with it the suggestion that I was entering my declining years (who else but those past their prime are asked to write the story of their life?) I was understandably flattered by the request. John must have thought I had contributed *something* to the struggle for animal rights; otherwise he wouldn't have asked me to write this story for his magazine.

The first thing I did was to re-read the previously published autobiographies. Then I set about the task of trying to create something that did not duplicate, either in style or tone, what already had been done. For good or ill, I have always wanted my work to be "original." "The Bird in the Cage: A Glimpse of My Life" is my attempt to be "original" in the genre of the autobiographical sketch. It is reprinted here with the knowledge and approval of John Stockwell. I thank him.

All of us engaged in the struggle for animal rights have a tendency to forget who we once were. Most of us once ate meat, for example, or unblinkingly dissected nonhuman animals in the lab during high school or college biology courses. Probably we went to a zoo or an aquarium and had a good time. Some of us hunted or fished and enjoyed that, too. The plain fact is, it is not just society that needs changing. The struggle for animal rights is also a struggle with the self. What we are trying to do is transform the moral zombie society would like us to be into the morally advanced being we are capable of becoming. All liberation movements have this common theme. That's only one of the ways our Movement resembles other rights movements of the past.

Society, after all, is happy with us when we go about the business of living without asking questions or causing trouble, doing nothing that challenges the status quo. We are loved if we are content to spend our dollars up to and, preferably, a good deal beyond what we are able to earn. Society loves an overspender, one who cares little about the hidden costs of cruising in the fast lane of consumerism.

Those who refuse to find total satisfaction in this role, those who think life has a moral significance that goes beyond how much we earn or own — which doesn't mean that we must earn or own nothing — are more or less out of step with the normal cadence of society at large. But all of us who resist the call to "Get in step!" with everyone else have our own private agenda of struggles. And that agenda isn't finished. We didn't get where we are overnight, and we aren't going to get where we want to be, where we aspire to be, tomorrow. Or the next day. Or the next. We *struggle* to advance, to progress, to come closer to the ideal we have for ourselves. And struggle we must. "No pain, no gain" is the way my coaches used to put it.

"The Bird in the Cage" is my attempt to convey something of the history of my personal struggle to find myself and to make the person I once was into the person I want to become. In it I reveal some facts about my life I wish I could deny. My hope is that by openly sharing my own limitations and temptations, my own weaknesses and shortcomings, I might help others come to acknowledge theirs.

The "others" I have in mind include both those who already are engaged in the struggle for animal rights as well as those who are not yet involved. For this latter group I hope the story of my struggle will strike a familiar, responsive chord. I hope you will see part of yourself in me and so come to understand how similar we are, despite appearances to the contrary. And I hope this recognition will play some role in helping you decide to join the struggle for animal rights.

As for those already involved in this struggle, I hope my candor will encourage candor on your part as well. The last thing animals need is another reason for exploiting or being indifferent to them. Yet this is precisely what aspirant "friends of animals" very often give: By being so doctrinaire and unfeeling in how we present our beliefs to nonbelievers, we often succeed in widening the gap between ourselves and those we wish to enlist in the cause. With "friends" like this, animals certainly don't need any enemies. Such "friends" *are* enemies. To drive people away from the Animal Rights Movement by what we say and how we say it is to aid the forces of oppression and exploitation. We must become *more human, more compassionate, more caring,* and *more honest* in our attempts to bring new people into our Movement. Only then are we likely to succeed.

Like many others, I fully believe that animal liberation is human liberation. The great task of those of us who presume to speak for the animals, to be the voice for the voiceless, is to embody the moral virtues of human liberation in our own person and to express them in our daily life. That is *our private struggle,* our struggle with our self. It goes hand in hand with the social struggle for animal rights. "The Bird in the Cage" attempts to tell one small chapter of this larger story.

Beginnings: A Kid of the Streets

I was born and raised in Pittsburgh, Pennsylvania —"the Burgh" as we who have lived there call it. Although I have not had a permanent residence there for more than thirty years I still consider Pittsburgh my home. The Burgh sets its roots deep in those who have known it. The City gets in your blood. You can't go away from home again.

The house where I spent the first fifteen years of my life fronted California Avenue, a busy thoroughfare on the city's North Side: four lanes of traffic, two trolley lines. It could get hectic. We *never* played ball on California Avenue. Beyond the traffic there was a sharp drop to a leveled space some fifteen feet below the street. A dozen train tracks sliced their way westward. You could not see the trains, either from the street or from the second story windows of our house. But their relentless presence was the most dominant aspect of daily life. This was before diesel engines. Everything was steam. That means coal-powered. The air was filled with great plumes of grayish white smoke and phosphorescent cinders that glowed in the night air. Passenger and freight trains hurried by, their whistles wailing throughout the day and all the night. Everywhere there was the crashing sound of cars being coupled and uncoupled on the Hump. Great lines of cars, hundreds at a time — freight and oil, flatbeds and cattle —were strung together by the skilled workmen. Twenty-four hours a day, seven days a week, every day of every month you heard the sound of heavy metal.

Everyone who lived along this sprawling artery that linked the coal mines of West Virginia to the steel mills of Pittsburgh belonged to the railroad. This was true even when, as in my family's case, no one worked for it. The soot and smoke invaded your eyes and ears, your nose and mouth, the elastic around your underwear and the clothes in your dresser. When you took a bath, a broad, dark black ring remained in the tub after you drained it, a reminder, lest one forget — how could one? — of the clanging world outside. My neighborhood was a child's paradise, a place where a kid could luxuriate in the steamy dirt of industrial urban living.

That neighborhood is all but gone now. The house where I was raised has been demolished. In fact the entire block of houses now is an open field, full of weeds and an occasional wildflower. Even the railroad is all but idle. Most of the houses that remain have been boarded up, condemned by the City as uninhabitable. When I drive through the old neighborhood today, grown silent and all but deserted, I am a ghost in a ghost-town. No one from my youth remains. Viewing the fading shrouds of what was once a vibrant neighborhood, where VJ Day and the Fourth of July were celebrated with patriotic fervor, where Jews mixed with gentiles, whites with blacks, every nationality with every other, no one would believe that there once were people here who loved these streets and narrow alleyways, the hard cement porches and creaking swings, the wooden City Steps winding to the hills above —those Steps where we kids spent Friday nights fantasizing about what we would do before and after the ten cent double feature at the Brighton Show on Saturday mornings. But love it I did. It always saddens me when I make my annual pilgrimage and see again the stilled emptiness progress has created.

As a kid of the streets the animals I knew were mostly the animals of the streets. Cats and dogs for the most part. But there were rats about — huge, menacing creatures that darted through the twisting alleys at night, their wild red eyes ablaze if caught in a beam of light. These were *Pittsburgh* rats — creatures who could eat through a plaster wall of an evening's diversion. And there were also horses. In those days vendors and junkmen rode four-wheeled wagons through the city, pulled by stoop-shouldered nags, weary creatures who were occasionally aroused from their dolorous fatigue by the high pitched clang of a trolley's bell or the crack of their master's whip. The horses' droppings left more or less permanent reminders of their having passed through. I never formed a close relationship with any of these horses, nor with the cattle and pigs who bellowed and squealed through the rough-sawn slats of the trucks and cattle cars en route to the slaughter house. Their cries fell on deaf ears in my case, blending as they did with the unbroken cacophony of urban sounds.

Tippy was another matter. One hundred percent mutt, she was an energetic black wisp of a dog with a small but clear tip of white at the very end of her tail. She was eager for affection and designed by nature to be free. Give her just the slightest crack in the gate and pow! —she was gone! Like a shot she was through the gate and around the corner. Her favorite adventure during these escapades was to roll ecstatically in the horse dung. What deep longing this primordial ritual fulfilled I do not know. But it was Nirvana for her while it lasted. I understand now that she lacked the space she needed to be the dog she was, and I see the shadow of her stunted life in those mournful looks on so many city dogs who live in close quarters. Still, Tippy did not want for warm human companionship. My fondest memory of her is when, wonder of wonders, thirty-six inches of snow fell on Pittsburgh in a matter of a few days. That kind of development suspends all the ordinary rules of behavior. Tippy spent long hours free to wander and play, and most of this time she spent with me and the other neighborhood kids. She knew a good time when she had one. Some photographs of those days remain. It is hard to tell who is happiest — Tippy or me.

Excursions: The Country

Not everything was urban in my youth. Along with my parents and sister I enjoyed fishing along the upper Allegheny River and berry and nut picking in the country. We also visited friends who had farms. Sometimes I stayed on after my parents and sister returned home; for a day, maybe a week-end, occasionally even a week. During these visits I lived with the farm, assaulted by the pungent odor of cow dung, outsmarted by the clever laying hens who knew inexperienced hands when they felt them. (I don't think I gathered a dozen eggs, total, throughout my youthful career.) The farm I knew best was small, devoted mainly to vegetables and flowers. In the winter plants were grown in a long, low-slung green house. It was bewildering to enter that luminous space, quiet as a church, feel the accumulated heat of the sun on a bitterly cold day and smell the sometimes dank, sometimes sweet odors of the plants. Without a doubt these were the most mysterious, most awesome moments of my youth, occasions when my experience was so full of inchoate meanings that I could not then, and cannot now, find the words to describe it. It was, I think, more a yearning than a fact I felt.

The few animals my parents' farming friends had were members of the extended family. They gave, and the others took - milk and eggs. But not life. When the cow was calfing someone slept in the barn, and on very cold nights kerosene heaters warmed the hen house. The animals had names — Bossie the cow, Bessie and Bert the chickens. Names like that. Not very imaginative, perhaps, but these names helped consolidate the bonds between the animals and their human caretakers. These farmers ate chicken, but never Bessie or Bert.

My guess is, many people of my generation had a farm like this in their childhood. Back then families took drives in the country on Sundays; farms were places people visited in those days. And for those who lacked this opportunity there were the stories: Henny Penny, Brer Rabbit, Black Beauty, and the breathtaking adventures of African explorers in *Our Weekly Reader* and of Tarzan on Saturday mornings at the movies. Through these windows we glimpsed a world apart from the piercing whistles of the steam engines in the night, heard alien sounds unlike the grating of huge steel wheels rolling across tracks worn sleek as silver. Urban kids of my generation and place were bred and raised on the machine, but we took sustenance in our real and imaginary commerce with the garden.

Some children understand early on what meat is. They realize that a roast or a pork chop or a chicken leg is a piece of dead animal. A corpse. I was not that precocious. Like most Americans I grew up unmindful of the connection between the food on my plate and the death of the creature it represents. The animals I knew personally, Tippy for one, and other dogs and cats in the neighborhood, I considered my friends. Even Bossie and Bert were objects of my affection. But I lacked the imagination then to see the connection between my fondness for these animals and the silent pieces of flesh that came from my mother's skillet or roaster. The human mind is remarkable for its ability to see the world in bits and pieces, each part disconnected from the rest like an expansive vista viewed through the narrow slits of a picket fence. It was not until much later in my life that the chronic idleness of my imagination was overwhelmed by the force of logic and the vicissitudes of experience.

Transition: The Burbs

Had my family remained on the North Side it is virtually certain that I never would have gone to college. People in that neighborhood grew up to work, not to study. My parents were products of that pattern. Neither finished the ninth grade. There was work to be done. Mouths to be fed. Education was a luxury. My parents were unable to pay the price.

My sister was different: She graduated from high school. But then the pattern took hold again. She went directly from the classroom to the workforce. A much better student than I was and natively much smarter, she was certain to have had a distinguished university career had she had the opportunity. Instead, she did clerical work in a nearby factory — a terrible loss I continue to lament to this day. And I? I was destined to follow my sister's lead. The duty of work called. It was not a matter of whether but where to get down to the task of making a living.

But then a momentous thing happened: We moved. To the suburbs. My parents decided that they had had it. That grime-filled heaven of my boyhood had been their hell for too long. We were *getting out!* No if's, and's, or but's. And I? I was fifteen, with deep roots in the friendships and places of my youth. If ever a child was resentful and full of anger, if ever hate took up lodging in a person's heart, these powerful emotions found a home in me. I was determined to be unhappy.

The world did not cooperate with my resolve. In the end the move was not as traumatic as I was bent on making it. I made new friends and soon found myself a part of a quite different environment. Many of my friends' parents had gone to college. They had professions — in medicine, the law, education. Their taste for culture trickled down to their children and, through them, to me. I soon found myself reading and talking about Camus and Andre Gide, discussing Nietzsche and Norman Mailer, listening to Bartok and Stravinsky. With my companions I drove into and around the Burgh to watch foreign and classic films. We debated God's existence and free will into the morning hours. For the first time in my life I began to write. Horrible fiction. Worse poetry. But I took the demands of the Muse seriously. And my teachers liked it. They told me I was a writer-in-the-making. They did not know the demands of the mines and the mills. Their life had found a place for the mind. And so had mine. But only an inch at a time.

Music was important. By my junior year in high school I was making a little money playing in big dance bands and in small combos. Glenn Miller. Ted Heath. Les Elgart. Harry James. Ellington. We played all the big bands' tunes and arrangements. And as for the combos: The AJQ. The MJQ.

Brubeck and Desmond. Gerry Mulligan. The (early) Miles Davis. We borrowed and played what we could. At small dances and parties. At wedding receptions. (Oh, the wedding receptions!) I was the lead Reed Man. I played any reed instrument in sight, but mostly clarinet and tenor sax. I doubt if I ever would have become a *really* good musician had I continued this career. But I did enjoy both the music and the camaraderie. In the civilian world the closeness of musicians may be the nearest thing to those legendary wartime friendships formed in foxholes.

After graduating from North Allegheny High School I went to college. This I did for a simple reason: It was what all my friends were doing. I then had only the faintest idea about what a college was. All I knew firsthand was that people "like me" went to one because — well, because that's what colleges were for. I was encouraged in this belief by the testimony of my teachers and other interested persons. I had a good but hardly outstanding academic record in high school (top tenth of my class, as I recall). Every Open House all my teachers told my parents the same thing: "Tommy could do *much* better if only he would *apply* himself." "Who couldn't?" I wondered at the time. And still do. But two people in particular — the late Reverend Luther Fackler, who was the minister of the Lutheran Church I attended, and Ralph Pannier, who in addition to being a near neighbor also taught my Sunday School class — these two men in particular encouraged me to give college a try. Perhaps in part it is because of their mutual involvement with the Church that I have never taken the power of religion lightly. Its power for the good, I mean.

Reverend Fackler had some more specific ideas in mind for me. And so did I. I thought I felt a "calling" for the ministry. But I was unsettled in my faith. Even before I went off to college I was unable to join in the recitation of the Apostles' Creed. The words stuck in my throat. Reverend Fackler told me not to worry. God would find me — but only if I stopped trying to find Him. This seems as unsound to me now as it did to me then. Any god who would find me only on the condition that I was not looking for him is a god not worth finding. That much hubris any human worthy of being created by God ought to have. I wrote an essay on this issue at the time, called "The Seeker", in which I affirmed this conviction. Neither perturbed nor distracted, Reverend Fackler counseled me not to worry overly much about my doubts. A true faith is measured by the depth of its temptations to deny, he said. As I was sorely tempted in the latter regard, off I went to college, like a modern Knight Errant, to find (or, perhaps, to be found by) the Divine Mind. I chose Reverend Fackler's college — Thiel College, a small liberal arts college affiliated with the Lutheran Church, an hour-and-a-half drive north of Pittsburgh. I applied to no other. Ralph Pannier and Mrs. Pannier were most supportive. My mother and father for a variety of reasons were less sure, as well they should have been. I was too. Folks from the North Side could smell trouble a mile away.

On The Banks of The Shenango: Thiel College

At the beginning college was everything my last years in high school had not been. I had a hard time making friends during my freshman year, despite playing (at 138 pounds) halfback on the football team. To say I "played" halfback in college may be — well, actually it is an exaggeration. I did letter in football (and in track and golf) in high school. College was a different league. I was in over my head and should have had enough sense to quit. But I didn't. It was not until my sophomore year that the Age of Wisdom dawned. I never played varsity football again. But even to this day I harbor the belief, as deep and unfalsifiable as any I have ever held, that I have good hands. You throw a ball near me and damned if I won't catch it!

Whatever Red Barber might write about my sporting life, my early academic career at Thiel was unspectacular. Mostly C's, with some B's and D's. Something like a 2.5 average on a 4.0 system. Before going off to college, as I mentioned earlier, my teachers encouraged me in the belief that I might someday be a writer. I was impressionistic enough to believe them. My teachers during my first two years at Thiel seemed to be intent upon demonstrating how reprehensible my high school teachers had been in fostering this belief in me and how stupid I had been in believing them. I received a more or less steady stream of D's and F's for my early compositions. This gave me second thoughts. Perhaps the Muse I was listening to spoke in dangling participles? Believe me, I thought long and hard about quitting more than once.

I even managed to flunk Spanish. Elementary Spanish at that. And I received a D in English composition. I was ready to chuck it. But then — and this was perhaps the most important event in my early years as a prodigal scholar — I stopped wearing socks. I wore only tennis shoes. Low-cut tennis shoes. This created a persona in whose presence I was quite comfortable. I was immediately viewed as the malcontented one. Different. The unfulfilled genius. The true, the only real intellectual Bohemian on campus. *That's* why my grades were lackluster. I was what then was called (the words were almost unspeakable at the time) a Beatnik. Like Allen Ginsberg. Like Jack Kerouac. What a relief this sartorial gesture towards self-identity was to me! Back then, where I went to college, *everyone* wore socks. Only some *really* rare and gifted person would dare to show his bare ankles in public. I liked this role. I began to believe in myself again. Today, given a more solid and independent self-image, I wear my socks everywhere I go. In public, that is.

To Avoid History: A Philosopher is Born

A crisis occurred during my junior year at Thiel. I was an English major at the time and to complete the required course of studies I was obliged to take a full year of English history as well as a year of United States and Pennsylvania history. This was like asking me to spend two years lounging on a bed of hot coals. Whatever talents and interests I may have had, the study of history did not nourish or answer them. Fortunately for me the forces of serendipity took charge of my life — not for the first or the last time.

Thiel was just about to introduce a new major in philosophy. I had taken a few philosophy courses by then and was pleased to discover that a subject actually existed where people discussed the questions I increasingly was inclined to ask on my own. In addition, my professors in philosophy showed an interest in me that was lacking in most of their counterparts in English. I would like to be able to say that I decided to major in philosophy because of my commitment to pursue Truth, whatever the cost. But the really decisive factor in my decision to change was far more banal. This new major in philosophy did not require any classes in history over and above those I had already taken. That much settled, the decision was easy. I was to be Thiel College's first-ever philosophy major. It was a decision made in the stars. During my senior year I was virtually a straight A student, barely graduating, however, because of a D for the second semester of Elementary Spanish. I doubt if I could do any better today. Many are called but few are chosen to Elementary Spanish.

By the time of my graduation from Thiel I had abandoned any desire I may once have had to prepare myself for the ministry. I didn't know where I was headed. My summer employment as a counselor at a YMCA camp was fulfilling. Another summer's apprenticeship in a local butcher shop was not. But this was not because I found butchering ethically intolerable. I had no moral qualms whatever about preparing the ground meat, making city-chicken, stocking the cold-cut section, fixing the minute steaks, or skewering the chickens for the rotisserie. My hands went deep into the corpses of animals, but I was stone deaf to their cries. I didn't like my apprenticeship because the work was too bloody hard, not because it was too bloody. My days in the butcher's trade were numbered. But not for anything like the right reasons.

As my graduation from Thiel approached I interviewed for a variety of jobs: selling insurance for Sears; serving as a Youth Counselor for a suburban branch of the YMCA; pursuing a career in marketing for H.J. Heinz. These interviews were glorious fiascos. It did not take me long to learn that I was a round peg trying to fit into square holes. And it didn't take my interviewers long to realize this either. I knew quite well what I did not want to do. The problem was to find the round hole that answered my needs and interests. I already had postponed a vocational decision four years beyond the point of anyone else in my family, including all of my relations on both sides. Not only was I the first one on either side to graduate from college, I was the first one to attend. I felt a great deal of anxiety about the need to do something with my life. People had been patient with me long enough. But what could a person do who had a bigger appetite for reading Kant than for selling Heinz's ketchup? That was the question whose answer eluded me.

If the idea of college was mysterious to me while I was in high school, the idea of graduate school was even more incomprehensible to me while I was in college. "What was a graduate school?" I wondered. "And what did a person do there?" I had only the foggiest idea. But as my job prospects dwindled (I was eliminated from consideration for the YMCA job because I didn't have the "right" ideas about where blacks belonged in the particular branch where I applied: They belonged *outside* I was told) — as my job prospects dwindled, I had to do something. And so it was that during the summer of 1960 I applied for admission to the Graduate School of Arts and Sciences at the University of Virginia, to continue my study of philosophy. Two weeks before the first class — (at least this is my recollection) — I received a letter informing me that I had been accepted "conditionally." This meant I was admitted but that my status would be re-evaluated on the basis of my work during the first semester. There was, after all, enough evidence of mediocrity on my college transcript to rattle anyone's confidence. Thank heavens my major professor at Thiel was a graduate of Virginia. Had it not been for the influence and guidance of Robert S. Bryan at this time I may well have ended up selling collision insurance for Allstate. And this is not the least of my many debts to Bob Bryan. His influence on me is surpassed only by that of my parents. He was, and continues to be, my mentor in the deepest, truest sense.

Still Unsettled: The University Years

My graduate career at Virginia began inauspiciously enough. I was blue collar in my background. The students I met all seemed to be Blue Blood in theirs. Virginia had no female students at the time and we Gentlemen (as we then were called) wore coats and ties to class. I had one suit and two ties. I was the kid without socks who spills soup on his pants to the delight of the country club set. Or so it seemed. I remember well a young man in my Plato seminar, a graduate of St. John's College in Annapolis, where the education consists of reading and discussing the Great Books, many of which I had never heard of let alone read. We were walking across the Grounds, having just passed the famous Rotunda designed by Thomas Jefferson, heading toward the Corner. Earlier in our seminar we had been discussing Plato's Theaetetus. I couldn't make much sense of the dialogue and was rash enough to say so. Others seemed not to find the material difficult. Stopping abruptly, my compatriot looked me squarely in the eye. Taking his pipe from his mouth (the smoking of a pipe, I discovered, was an essential mark of an educated Gentleman, one I tried to acquire, albeit unsuccessfully) and speaking with an affected British accent, he said, "Regan, you *strike* me as a man to whom it will *not* be difficult to say good-by come the end of your first and, dare I say, your *only* semester." Then he placed his pipe back in his mouth and walked away, leaving me transfixed on the spot where I stood.

I was shattered. Here I was, a kid off Pittsburgh's streets, trying to make an honest go of it at Mr. Jefferson's University. And here was this J. Press son-of-privilege putting me in my place, telling me that I didn't belong. And who was I to deny that he was right? Didn't I think his very thoughts myself? Socially and intellectually this was the lowest point of my life. It took me months to begin to regain any semblance of self-confidence. But in time I did, and though I am not a particularly vengeful or spiteful person I must confess that I took more than a little pleasure when, at the end of my first semester, I was invited to continue my studies in philosophy while my solemn colleague from St. John's was not. I thought of it then, and I think of it now, as a small but real victory for the working class.

My record at Virginia was good but not great. Some B's; mostly A's. I have the deepest affection for the teachers who taught me during the years I was there, and I have nothing but the most profound respect for the ideals The University embodies. I count myself very lucky indeed for having had the opportunity to pass through its corridors. I am the sort of person who is quietly loyal to institutions, not only people. Though I do not belong to anything as formal or social as a chapter of the Alumni Association I like to think of my efforts as a teacher and philosopher as my quiet way of trying to repay The University for its patient investment in me. Doors could have been closed that were opened. I shall never forget this. To this day one of my favorite quotes is from Jefferson; it is inscribed on the facade of the building where my seminars in philosophy were held. "Here we are not afraid to follow truth wherever it may lead," it reads, "or to tolerate the possibility of error, so long as reason is left free to combat it." That sentiment *is* The University in my mind, and nothing better captures my own sense of what the spirit of rational inquiry is or should be.

But lest it seem that I slight my debts to Thiel I must cite another, quite different, but no less true and important sentiment one will find inscribed on that College's sun dial. Roughly translated from the Latin it reads: "Perhaps in the future these things will appear beautiful." I cannot think of this observation without experiencing an involuntary shudder, as when one thinks one sees a dead friend in a crowd. The sun dial's message is right: Time does soften the harsh edges of past places and events. And that is not the only truth Thiel College gave me.

Moral Innocence: Animals Come and Go

In the Spartan, no-nonsense regimen of Thiel and the more refined ambiance of Virginia, animals were all but absent. The University had some legendary dogs — legendary largely for their proclaimed accomplishments as drinkers. (Back then students at UVA took pride in their well-deserved reputation as the biggest drinkers around.) Perhaps the story is apocryphal but one dog (Jock was his name, I think) was reputed always to have lifted his leg on the opponent's goal post at half-time during football games. And (so the story went) some two thousand people attended Jock's funeral, the dog having been killed (suitably enough, it was thought) while chasing a beer truck through the streets of Charlottesville. All this was part of the oral tradition at The University. No one I knew thought for a moment that there was anything morally dubious about getting a dog drunk or finding it *really funny* that old Jock would get himself killed by a truck filled with Budweiser. That I also found the story amusing at this time is symptomatic of those deeper, unarticulated beliefs I then had regarding animals, both about what they are and about how they should be treated.

The same insensitivity I showed towards Jock's fate I

exhibited in the face of a first year medical student's emotional anguish. At the beginning of my studies at Virginia I had a room in a spotless older home only a few minutes walk from the Grounds. In the room next to me lived the med student, a tough looking, broad-chested Polish Jew from New Jersey, very streetwise, very determined to get ahead with his career. Even so, he did not like what he was required to do to a dog in his class in surgery. He described to me how he broke the poor animal's leg and then set it, only to break and set it again. Throughout her long, painful ordeal the loyal animal greeted his arrival with a wag of her tail and even licked the very hands that had injured her. In the end, after he had studied one or another thing about her treatment and recovery, he was required to "euthanize" the dog. It did not sit well with him. He thought it cruel and unnecessary. He wanted to speak out, to object, but he lacked the courage. He wondered what sort of human being he was or would become. He even questioned whether he should make a career of medicine. In all this I believe he was as sincere as any man can be. It hurt him to hurt another, even a dog.

For my part I was too much involved in understanding Plato's Theaetetus and withstanding the insults of my peers to find time to empathize much with this medical student, let alone with the dog. I wish I could say that my ethical sensitivities regarding animals always have been highly developed. The sad truth is, they have not. The story about this dog bothered me no more and no less than the story about Jock. Animals were not on my moral map.

Among the truly major blessings in my life was my marriage to my wife Nancy on June 17, 1961. We remain indissolubly wedded, committed to our mutual growth. We are of course radically different people now than we were when we first met back in my sockless days at Thiel, and perhaps it is as much a matter of luck as it is of our love for one another that we have managed to develop in ways that have brought us closer together rather than driving us farther apart. Sometimes we even seem to *look* alike, impossible though this is — she of Lithuanian and Austrian blood, her face showing the strong beauty of her Eastern European ancestry, I of sturdy Irish stock, ruddy of complexion, stump-nosed. How very fortunate we are to have settled permanently into one another. There is so much more one can do with one's life after the questions of a proper mate and companion have been answered once and for all.

Early on in our marriage we purchased a miniature poodle. We called him "Gleco", after the name of a company we drove past every day en route to and from Charlottesville. Nancy was an instructor in Special Education, teaching retarded children in the public schools. I was taking my graduate seminars. We lived in two rooms on the second floor of an older farm house about thirteen miles from The University. The landlady was a strong-willed but friendly Southern woman who lived alone, having raised all her children after her husband, without any warning and so to everyone's surprise, committed suicide one Saturday morning. With a shotgun. She allowed her handyman to graze a few head of cattle on her pasture. Once, after a calf had been taken from his mother (I did not know what had happened at the time), I approached her because of the mournful cries of the mother. All through one night and into the next day the poor animal moaned and groaned. Surely, I told our landlady, the animal must be dying or at least be very sick. Shouldn't we do something to help her? Shouldn't we at least call the vet? Always the gentlewoman, our landlady permitted my city ignorance to pass without making much over it. Mothers worry over their children, she explained. The cow was calling out for her lost child. It was that simple. There was no need to do anything. She would forget her loss in time. As usual this sturdy twig of a woman was right. The following day the mother grazed contentedly. The next time I heard these same cries I understood what they meant, only this time I thought them rather a nuisance. I remember shouting out the window at the grieving mother, telling her to shut up. I had important work to do and she was bothering me.

Like so many newly married couples who acquire a pet, we treated Gleco as our substitute child. We took him everywhere we could, fretted over his every sign of unhappiness, felt guilt-ridden because we had to leave him alone during most days. For his part Gleco became a loyal but in some ways an always independent companion. There was something of the cat in him — a trace of aloofness beneath the surface sheen of his ordinary congeniality. Certainly he refused to be taught to heel and the rest of it, and his frequent displays of unbridled destructiveness when we left him alone made every return home suspenseful. "What *could* Gleco have done today?" Nancy and I wondered as we climbed the stairs and opened the door to our rooms. What he did on some days was to rip the bed apart, devour the sofa cover, tear the bottom out of the overstuffed armchair, and litter the logs from the fireplace to kingdom come. He never cared overly much about pleasing us. But he loved us just the same, and we loved him. His subsequent death helped change my life irreversibly.

The War: Fiddling My Profession

My education at Virginia was more or less typical of the time. "Analytic philosophy" was the dominant approach to the discipline in places with a heavy British influence, and Virginia's philosophy department certainly had a heavy British influence during my student years. "Animal rights" was not so much as mentioned. Probably it would have been swept out of the room if it had been. But neither were abortion, or euthanasia, or world hunger. The ruling preoccupation in moral philosophy, which is where my interests naturally led me, concerned questions about the proper analysis of concepts. My spirit bent to conform itself to what my teachers required. I wrote my Master's Thesis on the concept of beauty and my Ph.D. Dissertation on the concept of goodness. As a true professional my concerns were strictly analytic; I inquired into the meaning of the words 'good' and 'beauty'. Not a single judgment about the goodness or beauty of anything fell from my pen. At that time and in that place it was not the business of a philosopher to take a moral or aesthetic stand on anything. To do so was beneath the intellectual dignity of the profession. I practiced what I heard preached.

After my graduation, when I embarked on my teaching career, my classes in moral philosophy initially mimicked those I had had as a graduate student. But I was never wholly satisfied with this way of doing moral philosophy. What had originally attracted me to the subject were my deep worries over what things are just and unjust, right and wrong, good and bad. And yet here I was teaching moral philosophy, and doing research in the field, in ways that required that I set these important questions aside. Perhaps I would have managed to leave them permanently behind me had it not been for a development over which neither I nor any other ordinary person had much control. Before any of us quite realized it America was at war in Vietnam. And that fact changed a great deal, including the direction of my own intellectual development.

The dilemma I faced at the time was quite simple. Every evening on the news I sat and watched people being killed. Americans and Vietnamese. Young men the age of most of my students. Women and children. And here I was, an educated moral philosopher, worrying about the meaning of the word 'right' and whether there is such a thing as the naturalistic fallacy. I could see myself fiddling with my profession while Vietnam burned. Something had to give. And since it was beyond my power to stop the war (though I worked politically to help end it),

I decided to approach things from the philosophical side. I began to think about how my training as a moral philosopher could be applied to the questions that were being asked about the war. Ought we to be there? Was the war a just war? Is violence ever justified? Once the logic of these questions took root in my mind they acquired a life of their own. I was along for the ride-of-ideas. Or so it now seems. As strange as it may sound, the immediate ancestor of my views about animal rights was my first crude attempt to come to terms morally with the war in Vietnam.

If I had to be more precise and try to fix a particular time when the ride-of-ideas began in earnest, I would say it was during the summer of 1972. It was then that I was the beneficiary of a Summer Grant from the National Endowment for the Humanities. My plan was to think about pacifism — the view that it is always wrong, no matter what the circumstances, to use violence, whether in self-defense or aggressively. The conclusion I reached then, and the one I still hold now, is that occasions can and do arise in which the individual is morally justified in using violence. To do so in some cases of course may be foolish, but it is not immoral just because imprudent. I was not then, and am not now, a pacifist.

Now, no one who sets out to think about violence and pacifism can do the work that needs to be done and not read Gandhi. And read him I did: hundreds and hundreds, even thousands of pages of his simple prose. This in itself was remarkable. I have never been an energetic reader. I envy people (my wife Nancy is one of them) who are. I wish I could be counted among their number. But I cannot. Especially during the past dozen years or so, when I have written more and more, I have been guilty of reading less and less. Except, as I say, in the case of Gandhi. I read him with enormous energy and dedication. Perhaps it was in part because of what Gandhi was and not only because of what he said that he exercised such an uncommon power over me. This simple, fragile, apparently unsophisticated man, against all the odds and contrary to every sensible expectation, became a major actor on the world's political stage, expressing in his own life the principles of love and justice he would have a free, independent India express in hers. How extraordinary! Even now I cannot help feeling that Gandhi was as close to many of the most important moral truths as any mortal is likely to be. The difference is, he managed to live them.

In any event it was during this particular period, during the summer of 1972, that Gandhi began to raise my consciousness about the place of animals in the moral scheme of things. His views on vegetarianism were both simple and of a piece with his more general views about right conduct. The practice of *ahimsa* (frequently translated "nonviolence") does not stop at the borders of one's own species. Morally we are called upon to minimize our casual role in the use of violence in the world at large, even when animals are the victims. And since we can lead an active, healthy life without either killing animals ourselves or partaking of the products of the slaughter performed by others, duty requires that we refuse to eat meat. We must be vegetarians. That in very simple terms is what Gandhi teaches.

Once I had digested it I could no longer look at the world in quite the same way. The meat on my plate now had an accusatory voice. It was Gandhi's. And it would not take my history of indifference as an answer.

As a piece of reasoning Gandhi's argument seemed unassailable. Give him his premises and you couldn't avoid his conclusion. The problem was, I was not prepared to give him his premises, one of which included his commitment to pacifism. And so I set myself the task of thinking about the moral status of vegetarianism in ways that did not rely on Gandhian pacifism. My first published

essay relating to animal rights, "The Moral Basis of
Vegetarianism", which was published in the *Canadian
Journal of Philosophy* in October 1975, is the tangible
result of the line of reasoning I began to investigate in the
summer of 1972 and which I completed early in the
summer of 1974. Looking back at the essay today I see
much in it I would change. I think the argument goes
badly wrong in a number of places, and the style is too
plodding. But I like the sense of rational determination
and fair-mindedness evident between the lines. The ride-
of-ideas had begun. There was no getting off.

I have emphasized the crucial role Gandhi played in
my intellectual and moral development. I remind myself
of it often. People enter the Animal Rights Movement
through many different doors and at very different stages
of their lives. In my case I entered through the door of the
written word. Perhaps it was natural, therefore, that my
first attempts at making a contribution to the Movement
would follow the logic of my own beginnings. Up to now
my dominant contribution has taken the form of written
work, some of which I have read in a variety of lecture-
settings, most of which I have simply published. I know
firsthand, from my encounter with Gandhi's work, what
power the written word can have in some cases, and I am
understandably gratified when, as happens more often
than I have had any reason to expect, people tell me that
my own written work has changed their lives. When this
occurs I feel as if I am passing on some of the Light
Gandhi gave to me. For those in the Movement who are
disdainful of "theory" and "philosophy" (and some people
in the Movement still fit this description) the steadily
growing number of people who enter the Movement
through the door of Ideas provides the most compelling
answer. In the long run it is the power of our ideas that will
make the most profound and lasting contribution to the
cause of justice for animals. Or so I believe.

The Death of a Friend:
The Imagination Awakens

But there was another event in my life that helped change it irrevocably, and this one had nothing whatever to do with philosophy or theory. This was an affair of the heart, not the head. And it also took place in that momentous summer of 1972.

Nancy and I, and our two children, Karen and Bryan, who then were one and five respectively, had taken a vacation at the beach. On the very day we returned home Gleco was killed — hit by a car while darting across a road. Whether the driver or the person in whose care we left Gleco was at fault will never be known. All that we knew at the time was that a dear friend was dead. Faced with that ugly fact, Nancy and I lapsed into a period of intense, shared grief. For days we cried at the mere mention or memory of Gleco's name, unable fully to articulate our sense of loss. Earlier that summer, while thinking about Gandhi and pacifism, I had encountered the rude question of the ethics of meat eating. Once severed from any essential connection with pacifism, and the rational arguments seemed to be there, I thought. My head had begun to grasp a moral truth that required a change in my behavior. Reason demanded that I become a vegetarian. But it was the death of our dog that awakened my heart. It was the sense of irrecoverable loss that added the power of feeling to the requirements of logic.

What Gleco's death forced upon me was the realization that my emotional attachment to that particular dog was a contingent feature of the world. Of *my* world. Except for a set of circumstances over which I had no control I would have loved some other dog (Jock, perhaps, or the poor creature at the mercy of the med student I knew). And given some other conditions over which I again had no control I would never have even known Gleco at all. I understood, in a flash it seemed, that my powerful feelings for this *particular* dog, for *Gleco,* had to reach out to include other dogs. Indeed, *every* other dog. Any stopping point short of every dog was, and had to be, rationally and emotionally arbitrary. And not just dogs, of course. Wherever in the world of animals there is a psychology with which to empathize, a personality whose welfare can be affected by what we do (or fail to do), there the feelings of love and compassion, of justice and protection must find a home. From this point forward my heart and head were one, a union. Philosophical argument can take the heart to the river, but perhaps it is only experience that can make it drink. The intellectual challenge before me was to try to make this sense of the world less vague and the grounds for accepting it rationally more compelling. That in general was the task I set myself and at which I worked more or less continuously during the next ten years of my life.

Comes the Revolution: Changes in Philosophy

"The Moral Basis of Vegetarianism" enjoyed a life beyond the usual grave of the professional journal. It was anthologized in a number of different collections of essays for use in courses in contemporary ethical issues. It became part of a trend, one that took discussions of animal rights into philosophy's classrooms. Whereas there was not a single philosophy course in which the idea of animal rights was discussed when "The Moral Basis of Vegetarianism" was completed, there now are perhaps a hundred thousand students a year discussing this idea today. Just in philosophy. A partial (but certainly not the whole) explanation of this revolutionary change lies in the solid classroom adoptions enjoyed by some of the books in which I have played an editorial role. These include *Matters of Life and Death* (1980), *Earthbound* (1983), *Just Business* (1983), and two books I co-edited with my colleague Donald VanDeVeer: *And Justice for All* (1982) and *Health Care Ethics* (1987). Differ though they do, each of these books includes discussions of animal rights. Their success has helped put "animal rights" in philosophy's classrooms where it belongs.

Along with this change in the presence of animal rights in courses in philosophy, philosophers themselves have brought about a significant change in our professional journals. When Peter Singer and I worked on the first edition of *Animal Rights and Human Obligations* (1976) our problem then was that there was too little good material by philosophers from which to choose. As we work on the revised and expanded second edition our problem now is that there is too much. Prestigious journals from around the world have devoted whole issues to discussions of animal rights: these include *Philosophy* (England), *Ethics* (USA), *Inquiry* (Norway), and *Etyka* (Poland). The rate of increase in professional essays published on animal rights must approximate the extraordinary rate of increase in the number of students who now discuss the idea. What we have witnessed during this period is nothing less than a revolution in how the idea of animal rights is perceived by a large, growing number of highly competent thinkers. The contribution this has made to the emerging but still fragile image of respectability the Animal Rights Movement currently enjoys is incalculable. Given even the most modest estimate, however, that contribution is enormous. Among the most gratifying things in my life is my knowledge that I have played some role, however small, in making this revolution happen. And this without firing a shot. Gandhi surely would have approved.

Other Work: Songs of Myself

In addition to the anthologies in which I served in an editorial capacity I also kept myself busy after 1972 by writing a number of essays for a largely professional audience. Some of these I was able to collect together in a volume of my own papers, *All That Dwell Therein: Essays on Animal Rights and Environmental Ethics* (1982). Whatever their philosophical shortcomings may be (and they are many), these essays chart the history of my struggle to find and articulate a rights-based understanding of the moral ties that bind us to other animals. The last word is not to be found in any of these papers. Each is a sketch at best. But each seems to me now to have been an essential step along the way to the view I was looking for.

That view is set forth in *The Case for Animal Rights* (1983). This work represents the fruit of more than a decade of hard thinking about the rights of animals. It comes as close as I shall ever come to getting at the deeper truths on which, in my view, the Animal Rights Movement stands or falls. It is a work of serious, methodical scholarship, written in the language of philosophy: "direct duties," "acquired rights," "utilitarianism," the whole lexicon of academic philosophy. It can be rough going for someone unfamiliar with the field. But I make no apologies for its difficulty. Physics is hard. In my view moral philosophy is harder. There already were enough books that pretended to make the questions of ethics, including how animals should be treated, easy. A new book, one that did not blink in the face of difficult ideas, was needed. Or so I thought. I made every attempt to make the hard ideas I discuss as accessible as possible. But no amount of effort can make hard ideas easy. On this score I am especially gratified by the number of people, including the book's toughest reviewers, who have praised *The Case* for its exemplary clarity.

The Case was conceived by me to be, and I continue to hope it will function as, an intellectual weapon to be used in the cause of animal rights. I wanted to give the lie, once and for all, to all those opponents of animal rights who picture everyone in the Movement as strange, silly, overly emotional, irrational, uninformed, and illogical. *The Case* is my attempt to ram these accusations down the throats of the uninformed, illogical, careless, irrational, strange, silly, and overly emotional people who make them. Ram them down their throats *nonviolently,* of course. I do retain this much of Gandhi's pacifism.

My view of *The Case's* utility is simply this: Unless or until the opponents of animal rights have read and understood its arguments, and unless and until they have rationally shown that the book's central conclusions are defective, they have not a rational leg to stand on. They speak without knowledge. They utter words without understanding. The demand should go out, at least for the present, that the exploiters of animals answer *The Case.* I harbor the hope that they will lack the ability to do so. Which is why I want the weapon used. It *can* be lethal. It pleases me to see that some people are beginning to recognize the range of the book's possible use. And its potential power.

I also am pleased, for different reasons, to see the increasing number of people who are beginning to recognize how my views differ fundamentally from Peter Singer's. As early as 1978 Singer denied, in print, that animals have rights. He even apologized for using the expression "animal rights" in his earlier writings, confessing that the use of this expression was nothing more than a "concession to popular rhetoric," something he said he "regretted." No one, it seems, paid attention. "Animal Rights" and "Peter Singer" became synonymous ideas in the minds of many people, even people in the Animal Rights Movement. I cannot begin to count the number of times I have sat through discussions or read essays in which my views regarding the rights of animals were attributed, not to me, but to Singer. I would be less than honest if I said this never bothered me. It has. Often. And a lot. But I have tried to hold my tongue and to acquire the virtue of patience — never easy for an Irishman! What pleases me now is that more and more people are beginning to recognize that the views they accept and want to see defended — tough-minded views about *animal rights* — are to be found in my work, not in Singer's. Intellectually and personally fewer things give me greater satisfaction. I want nothing more for my ideas than what they are due. But I also want nothing less.

Liberation: Out from Under
The Need to Say More

The process of writing *The Case* was remarkable. I worked as many as eighteen hours a day for almost a full year, during which time I again was the fortunate recipient of a Fellowship from the National Endowment for the Humanities. I am a compulsive rewriter. I doubt if there is a single sentence in *The Case* that wasn't recast at least once. Maybe even twice. Physically, the work was exhausting. Psychologically, it was invigorating. I never was tempted to abandon the project. Once under way I never veered off course. I was never depressed or displeased about how the book was going. Each day was too short, not too long. I was absolutely filled with, and by, the process of writing. I came away from my year's work on the book with the conviction that I have the *temperament* of a writer. Whether I have any of the necessary skills is another issue. How lucky those people are who are able to make an adequate living at this craft. How courageous are those who try.

There is another point about the process of writing *The Case* I should mention. When I started the book I did not hold the "radical" conclusions I reach in the final chapter. At the beginning I was against causing animals "unnecessary" suffering in scientific research, for example, but I was not against causing them "necessary" pain. Like Singer now, I was not an abolitionist then. What was perhaps the most remarkable, exciting part of working on *The Case* was how I was led by the force of reasons I had never before considered to embrace positions I had never before accepted, including the abolitionist one. The power of ideas, not my own will, was in control, it seemed to me. I genuinely felt as if a part of Truth was being revealed to me for the first time. Of course I do not want to claim that anything like this really happened. Here I am only describing how I experienced things. And how I experienced them, especially towards the end of the composition of the book, was qualitatively unlike anything else I have ever experienced. It was intoxicating. It was as close to anything like a sustained religious or spiritual revelation as I have ever experienced. Or am ever likely to experience again.

The publication of *The Case* marked the end of one phase of my life and the beginning of several others. Having got the book out of my system I was liberated from the need to write anything else of a technical nature about animal rights. That work is done. Behind me. With only a few possible exceptions, whatever other written contributions I may make to the Movement will be different. Before *The Case* my audience consisted largely of my peers in philosophy. In future it normally will be the public. A simple, undemanding book on animal rights is the next big project I am likely to undertake. I am eager to get on with it.

No Time for Rest: New Beginnings

This newly acquired freedom from the need to do technical philosophy has allowed me to strike out in a variety of new directions. During the academic year 1984-85 I had the great good fortune to be a Fellow at the National Humanities Center, a beneficiary for a third time of funds from the National Endowment for the Humanities. This time I wrote a book on the English philosopher George Edward Moore — *Bloomsbury's Prophet: G.E. Moore and the Development of His Moral Philosophy* (1987). This book doesn't so much as *mention* the word 'animal'. It is a contribution to intellectual history. Without my saying so the book makes it clear that Tom Regan, the philosopher, is in a new line of business.

I worked no less hard on this book than I did on *The Case for Animal Rights,* and I enjoyed the process of writing (and rewriting!) just as much. I wanted to write a book about a philosopher that was unlike any other book ever written about a philosopher, just as I had previously wanted to write a book about animal rights that was similarly unique. I think my book about Moore is unique in the ways I hoped it would be. Whether others think it is a really good book remains to be seen. I like it tremendously myself. After a year's hard work with a book you and it become good friends.

This new path I am exploring as a scholar does not mean that I have abandoned academic and other work that relates to the Animal Rights Movement. On the contrary my involvement increases steadily, so much so that my life as a creative scholar in other areas runs the risk of becoming something of a hobby. My solution to this problem at this point in time is to do more editorial work. Temple University Press has asked me to be the general editor of a series of scholarly books in moral philosophy, and I have also agreed to be the General

Editor of a fourteen volume series of college texts for Random House. Work on these two projects should be enough to keep me off the streets at night for the foreseeable future. I don't think I'll run out of things to do in my capacity as a scholar outside the field of animal rights.

As important as these projects are the new steps I am taking in relation to the Movement are even more so. One question those in the Movement must ask themselves every day is, "How do we attract new people to the cause?" My answer is that we must try to reach new or neglected constituencies. And there is no question in my mind that one of the most neglected constituencies is religion. Both institutional and academic. In the past three years or so I have begun to try to help correct this oversight. And so have others. There is another revolution coming. And it's going to be a big one.

An early sign of change was the July 1984 conference, which I was invited to help organize and chair, on Religious Perspectives on the Use of Animals in Science, sponsored by the International Association Against Painful Experiments on Animals. The proceedings of this conference have been published under my editorship by Temple University Press in 1986. The title: *Animal Sacrifices*. That is a first step in the process of getting animal rights into religion's classrooms and journals. A second step will be the publication of a collection of readings *(The Place of Animals in the Christian Faith)* on which Andrew Linzey and I currently are at work. When this anthology becomes available it will help generate the kind of change in academic religion that the publication of *Animal Rights and Human Obligations* helped make possible in the case of academic philosophy ten years ago.

But animal rights must get a fair hearing in our places of worship, not only our classrooms and professional quarterlies in religion. Toward that end I have written and directed a film, "We Are All Noah", for use in

Sunday School classes, discussion groups and the like, in both the Christian and Jewish religious communities. Priests, rabbis, ministers, and interested lay people appear in the film and have helped in other ways. People *inside* the families of religion, not "animal crazies" outside them, show what factory farming is and explain why a conscientious religious person cannot ignore this brutal exploitation of God's creatures any longer. And the same theme is played in the case of the use of animals in science, of hunting and trapping, and of pet abuse. Now that "We Are All Noah" is available (and information about its availability can be obtained from the Culture & Animals Foundation, 3509 Eden Croft Drive, Raleigh, NC 27612) the Animal Rights Movement finally has an appropriate vehicle for raising the animal rights issue in houses of worship. How do we attract new people to The Movement? *Animal Sacrifices, The Place of Animals in the Christian Faith,* and "We Are All Noah" are among my ways of trying to answer this question in the case of religion. Other people are offering other answers. The cumulative effect of the efforts of many will rouse that sleeping giant, religion. And the Movement will never be the same.

But we must not stop here. The Movement must reach out to other neglected constituencies and find new ways of raising the public's consciousness. We ourselves must become more aware of the deep cultural roots the Movement has — in philosophy and poetry, art and sculpture, music and dance. And we must add to this body of cultural resources in ways that will help educate the public both about the plight of the animals for whom we labor and about the character of those of us who labor for them.

The need to move on these fronts is what underlies the formation of The Culture and Animals Foundation (CAF), a nonprofit organization that raises and distributes money to fund three programs.

1. *The Research Program.* CAF funds selected scholarly research in the arts and humanities which promises to add significantly to our knowledge of artists and thinkers whose work expresses positive concern for animals.

2. *The Creativity Program.* CAF funds creative endeavors by contemporary artists and scholars in the humanities whose work is or will be expressive of positive concern for animals.

3. *The Performance Program.* CAF organizes and funds, at its discretion and subject to available monies and material, the performance and exhibition of artistic works, and the presentation of the fruits of humanistic scholarship, that have been funded by The Research or The Creativity Programs.

Except for normal operating expenses CAF does not allocate any of its funds for purposes other than those described in the above.

The Board of CAF is deliberately small. Dean John Bowker of Trinity College, Cambridge University, is Vice President. Carol Aycock, former Director of the History of Theater Program, Wake Forest University, is Secretary-Treasurer. I currently serve as President. I have never been so much as an official *member* of an animal organization let alone an officer of one. I have valued my independence, never wanting to be a part of a political divisiveness that has sometimes characterized The Movement. That I would *create* CAF says something about how crucially important I believe its role in the Movement is.

It is too early to say if CAF will succeed. We do know this, however: The work of scholars in philosophy has revolutionized the seriousness of animal rights in that discipline's journals and classrooms. And that mood of seriousness has flowed beyond these rooms and pages to the world outside. There is no reason why the same thing cannot happen in other areas — in literature and legal theory, in painting and dance, in religion and music. CAF will help make this change possible. And it will accelerate the Movement's rate of growth. We need to take charge of these things ourselves, not wait for others to do this for us. Because of the support of the National Endowment for the Humanities and my university, North Carolina State University, I have been one of the very few lucky ones who have had the necessary financial support to do the kind of scholarly work that is essential if the Movement is to go forward. CAF will see to it than many more scholars and artists receive the support they deserve. Their work will speak to neglected constituencies and help change the image of the movement. For *we* are the voice of what is best in our culture. It is time the public found this out.

Into the Breach: Radicalizing the Movement

Of late I have begun to take a few other steps to help add to the Movement's strength. I believe the campuses of America's colleges and universities are a neglected constituency. I think they are ready to be "radicalized" in ways that remind one of the "student unrest" of the sixties. Our students today suffer from pent-up idealism. They want — and need — to be a part of something good. And this good thing will be better in their view if it is something their parents did not champion before them. The present generation of students wants and needs a *new* cause — *their* cause. I sense this in my daughter Karen and my son Bryan. And in their friends. They are waiting for the right cause to capture their abundant energy and imagination. I have no doubt that we can help them choose the cause of animal rights. I have lent my hand to early efforts to get this process started. I shall do more in the future.

Mention of student unrest in the sixties hearkens back to the Vietnam War, and that in turn calls up the name of Gandhi and nonviolent means of protest: boycotts, sit-ins and the like. I believe the time has come for the Animal Rights Movement to go the route of every other successful movement for social justice. Our problem is not that we have too many nonviolent animal activists who are willing to go to jail in the name of animal rights; our problem is that we have too few. People in leadership roles in the Movement must take the initiative and "radicalize" others by becoming civil disobedients themselves. True to my Gandhian lineage I encourage principled reliance on nonviolence. Which does not mean inaction. (When I joined the other civil disobedients in the peaceful (and successful) occupation at NIH in June 1985 I certainly did not think that I was *doing nothing!*) The day *may* come when we are able to fill the jails with morally conscientious animal activists who care enough to practice civil disobedience. I hope so. The Movement is unlikely to triumph if that day never dawns.

Other major constituencies cry out for attention. The Animal Rights Movement is only one part of the larger movement for social justice. It must begin to align itself with other parts — with the Peace Movement, for example, and the Greens; with organizations trying to find missing children and those working to help battered wives; and with still other groups who labor for justice for East Asians, Blacks, Chicanos, and other minorities. Representatives of these and other groups must be a part of our Movement's campaigns and rallies. And the same is true of the working class. I am a product of that class and have deep loyalties and affection for those who comprise it. The Movement must learn how to reach out to those decent men and women. Although I myself am making a major effort on the cultural front through CAF's programs, I do not think the Animal Rights Movement will be a truly powerful political force until we have labor marching with us. I hope to start the process of blue collar involvement. Soon. There is so much to do, so little time to do it. The future waits.

Nature Rebels: Understanding Weakness

Probably everyone who reflects on the life he or she has lived up to a given point in time is struck by how chancy it all seems. Consider my case. Suppose my family had never moved from Pittsburgh's North Side: Would I have gone to college? Very unlikely. But even if I had, would I have gone to *Thiel* College? More unlikely still. And that means that in all probability I would not have met either Bob Bryan or my wife. How very unlikely then, that I would have gone to the University of Virginia to study philosophy. Or grown into the person who wrote *The Case for Animal Rights* and is now thinking of ways to create new points of entry into the Movement for Animal Rights. I can never think of my past without being overwhelmed by how much of what has happened to me (and this includes the very best things) was due to factors quite beyond my control. I try to remember this when I meet people whose ideas and values differ significantly from my own. "There but for a series of contingencies go I," I think. This helps me in my battle against self-righteousness. And in my efforts to be patient with people who are just entering the Movement as well as those who currently are outside it. How little of what we are and what we will become is within our power to control.

And so it is that I look back uncertainly at that self I once was. I see the boy playing on Pittsburgh's streets, unmindful of the aged, mistreated mare pulling an overloaded wagon of junk and old iron, the master's whip whistling angrily over her weary head. I watch the teenager running his hands over a butchered side of beef without giving it a second thought. And I observe the aspirant Virginia Gentleman listening indifferently to another's moral anguish concerning a solitary dog used in practice surgery, his own mind preoccupied with loftier worries about Plato's theory of Forms. And in every case I wonder, not superficially but down to the very depths of my being, if there is not the slightest hint, the most miniscule portent, of what my future was to be, or where my thought would and must lead me. Is it all a matter of luck? Of chance? Of accident? Was there nothing in me that directed my growth from within?

There is, perhaps, one hint of my destiny all but hidden in the blur of my boyhood memories. I was born with what has come to be called a "lazy" or "weak eye." Other names for my condition are "cock-eyed" or "cross-eyed." It is not a condition a boy could easily ignore. Others, especially one's antagonists, delighted in reminding one of the defect. I am told that some Native American peoples viewed crossed-eyes as positively beautiful and thought that anyone who was blessed with this condition must be very special to the gods. I do not know whether this is true. I do know it was not part of the oral traditions current on the streets of Pittsburgh during my youth. I was terribly self-conscious and wore my glasses constantly. This merited the name "four-eyes" which, though not a confidence booster in its own right, was less devastating than "cock-eyed!" Corrective surgery, which is now routine for very young children with a lazy eye, was not in vogue back then. What was recommended were exercises, and these were done with the aid of a mechanical device at the opthalmologist's office. And so off I would go every now and again to try to strengthen my weak eye.

The device was constructed as follows. If you looked

through the right lens, you saw a bird. And if you looked through the left lens, you saw a cage. People with normal eyes who looked through both lenses at the same time saw the bird imposed on the cage, which gave the appearance that the bird was in the cage. I saw things differently. In my case, because of my weak left eye, the bird always appeared to the right and slightly below the cage. Sometimes, when I concentrated as hard as I could, the bird seemed to move closer to the cage. But try as I might I never could get the thing right: I never could see the bird in the cage.

Today, thinking back on what at the time appeared to be a serious failure on my part, I glimpse the one deeply mysterious suggestion of where I was headed with my life, the one possible portent of what I would — and must —become. And do. Try as I might my nature would not permit me to see the bird in the cage. Something in me rebelled against having things this way. Others saw the bird as captive. I could only see the bird as free. And that, in its way, is a prophetic metaphor of what I have become.

My fate, one might say, is to help others see animals in a different way — as creatures who do not belong in cages. Or in leghold traps. Or in skillets. Or in any of the other cruel inventions of the human mind. Perhaps, indeed, there is in everyone a natural longing to help free animals from the hands of their oppressors — a longing only waiting for the right opportunity to assert itself. I like to think in these terms when I meet people who are not yet a part of the Animal Rights Movement. Like Socrates I see my role in these encounters as being that of the midwife, there to help the birth of an idea already alive, just waiting to be delivered. I have some sense that this is true in my case; the early evidence is there in my natural inability to see the bird in the cage. And yet how long it took for the idea contained in that "failure" to be born!

When viewed in this way, and notwithstanding the painful evidence to the contrary — the many instances of my own indifference to animal suffering, some of which I have been obliged to confess on this occasion — when viewed in this way I think I sense that all has not been chance or accident in my life. When viewed in this way I think I see that the child I once was, *is* the father of the man I have become. I sense that I have found my proper destiny. My place. My soul. Or possibly this has been given to me. Perhaps Reverend Fackler was right after all.

2

The Case for Animal Rights

Once upon a time there was a widespread caricature of those who spoke out for compassionate treatment of nonhuman animals. "Little old ladies in tennis shoes" was the description. That never was true of the great majority of animal rights advocates, and it certainly is not true of most of us today. Still, there *were* some "little old ladies" whose concern for animals was anything but little and whose determined efforts should never be overlooked or undervalued. Myself, I speak out on behalf of these wonderful human beings every chance I get. We wouldn't be where we are today if they hadn't worked as hard as they did in the past. We owe them much.

Like the derogatory expressions "animal lovers" and "sentimentalists," the "little old ladies in tennis shoes" caricature is part of a defensive syndrome characteristic of those in the business of exploiting nonhuman animals. Language is a powerful weapon, both for good and for ill and the rhetoric of the animal exploiters is no exception. By painting the advocates of animal rights with a broad verbal brush, ignoring the real differences that exist among the great variety of people involved in the struggle for animal rights, the exploiters stand to gain a good deal more than they have lost. "Animal weirdos," "animal crazies," "cranks," "lunatic fringe," "extremists" — these are today's equivalents of the "little old ladies in tennis shoes" of yesterday. Each is painfully familiar.

I'm from the old school myself, at least in this sense: I still think that the best defense is a good offense. What this means in the present case is to show, in a calm, reasoned, and informed way, that the truth lies on the side of animal rights. And I mean "animal rights" in the strongest sense, the sense in which, for example, recognition of their rights must lead to the conclusion that *all* research on healthy animals, conducted in the name of what is beneficial to human beings, must end. If I have made any lasting contribution to the Animal Rights Movement, it is most likely to be found in my work in this area, both my philosophical essays (collected in my 1982 book, *All That Dwell Therein: Essays on Animal Rights and Environmental Ethics)* and my detailed examination of the issues in *The Case for Animal Rights,* published in 1983.

These books differ in significant ways, but there is one thing that characterizes both: Both almost totally lack emotion. The issues are set out and examined in a dispassionate, rigorous, almost clinically detached manner. And this for a very good reason. Our "best defense" against the charge of being excessively sentimental and emotional is to disdain all such appeals *and still show that the case for animal rights can be made*. Whether I have been successful or not, this is what I have tried to do in my philosophical work. I am sustained by my belief that this work has done some good in the past and will do more good in the future.

Most of that work makes for difficult reading. It demands a great deal of patience and perseverance to work one's way through all the arguments and counter arguments. Comparatively few people are likely to have the necessary staying power. The following essay, also entitled "The Case for Animal Rights", is intended for those who want to have a clear sense of the intellectual foundation of the Animal Rights Movement but who choose not to suffer through the book of the same title. The essay, one might say, is the equivalent of a set of Cliffs Notes for the book. For those wanting the missing details, I can do no better than to recommend a good look at the book.

The main point I would emphasize is this simple one: Reason, not just emotion, is on the side of animal rights. For those who would deny this, our challenge should be no less simple and always the same: Show where the case for animal rights goes wrong, and show this without making unsupported appeals to emotion or by disdaining the highest standards of an unsentimental logic. We have met the challenge to be cool and logical. Or so I believe. Until our opponents are able to do as well — and none has succeeded to date, despite many attempts — we have every reason to believe that we have truth, not just feeling, on our side. It is our opponents, not those of us who struggle for animal rights, who are "emotional." In some dim sense, I think that they realize the game is over and that they have lost. And they don't like it. Speaking for myself, I must say, simply, I do.

"The Case for Animal Rights" originally appeared in *In Defense of Animals,* edited by Peter Singer (Oxford: Basil Blackwell, 1985), and is reprinted here with the kind permission of both the editor and the publisher.

I regard myself as an advocate of animal rights — as a part of the animal rights movement. That movement, as I conceive it, is committed to a number of goals, including:

- the total abolition of the use of animals in science;

- the total dissolution of commercial animal agriculture;
- the total elimination of commercial and sport hunting and trapping.

There are, I know, people who profess to believe in animal rights but do not avow these goals. Factory farming, they say, is wrong — it violates animals' rights — but traditional animal agriculture is all right. Toxicity tests of cosmetics on animals violates their rights, but important medical research — cancer research, for example — does not. The clubbing of baby seals is abhorrent, but not the harvesting of adult seals. I used to think I understood this reasoning. Not any more. You don't change unjust institutions by tidying them up.

What's wrong — fundamentally wrong — with the way animals are treated isn't the details that vary from case to case. It's the whole system. The forlornness of the veal calf is pathetic, heart wrenching; the pulsing pain of the chimp with electrodes planted deep in her brain is repulsive; the slow, torturous death of the raccoon caught in the leg-hold trap is agonizing. But what is wrong isn't the pain, isn't the suffering, isn't the deprivation. These compound what's wrong. Sometimes — often — they make it much, much worse. But they are not the fundamental wrong.

The fundamental wrong is the system that allows us to view animals as *our resources,* here for *us* — to be eaten, or surgically manipulated, or exploited for sport or money. Once we accept this view of animals — as our resources —the rest is as predictable as it is regrettable. Why worry about their loneliness, their pain, their death? Since animals exist for us, to benefit us in one way or another, what harms them really doesn't matter — or matters only if it starts to bother us, makes us feel a trifle uneasy when we eat our veal escalop, for example. So, yes, let us get veal calves out of solitary confinement, give them more space, a little straw, a few companions. But let us keep our veal escalop.

But a little straw, more space and a few companions won't eliminate — won't even touch — the basic wrong that attaches to our viewing and treating these animals as our resources. A veal calf killed to be eaten after living in close confinement is viewed and treated in this way: but so, too, is another who is raised (as they say) 'more humanely'. To right the wrong of our treatment of farm animals requires more than making rearing methods 'more humane'; it requires the total dissolution of commercial animal agriculture.

How we do this, whether we do it or, as in the case of animals in science, whether and how we abolish their use — these are to a large extent political questions. People must change their beliefs before they change their habits. Enough people, especially those elected to public office, must believe in change — must want it — before we will have laws that protect the rights of animals. This process of change is very complicated, very demanding, very exhausting, calling for the efforts of many hands in education, publicity, political organization and activity, down to the licking of envelopes and stamps. As a trained and practising philosopher, the sort of contribution I can make is limited but, I like to think, important. The currency of philosophy is ideas — their meaning and rational foundation — not the nuts and bolts of the legislative process, say, or the mechanics of community organization. That's what I have been exploring over the past ten years or so in my essays and talks and, most recently, in my book, *The Case for Animal Rights*. I believe the major conclusions I reach in the book are true because they are supported by the weight of the best arguments. I believe the idea of animal rights has reason, not just emotion, on its side.

In the space I have at my disposal here I can only

sketch, in the barest outline, some of the main features of the book. It's main themes — and we should not be surprised by this — involve asking and answering deep, fundamental moral questions about what morality is, how it should be understood and what is the best moral theory, all considered. I hope I can convey something of the shape I think this theory takes. The attempt to do this will be (to use a word a friendly critic once used to describe my work) cerebral, perhaps too cerebral. But this is misleading. My feelings about how animals are sometimes treated run just as deep and just as strong as those of my more volatile compatriots. Philosophers do — to use the jargon of the day — have a right side to their brains. If it's the left side we contribute (or mainly should), that's because what talents we have reside there.

How to proceed? We begin by asking how the moral status of animals has been understood by thinkers who deny that animals have rights. Then we test the mettle of their ideas by seeing how well they stand up under the heat of fair criticism. If we start our thinking in this way, we soon find that some people believe that we have no duties directly to animals, that we owe nothing to them, that we can do nothing that wrongs them. Rather, we can do wrong acts that involve animals, and so we have duties regarding them, though none to them. Such views may be called indirect duty views. By way of illustration: suppose your neighbor kicks your dog. Then your neighbor has done something wrong. But not to your dog. The wrong that has been done is a wrong to you. After all, it is wrong to upset people, and your neighbor's kicking your dog upsets you. So you are the one who is wronged, not your dog. Or again: by kicking your dog your neighbor damages your property. And since it is wrong to damage another person's property, your neighbor has done something wrong — to you, of course, not to your dog. Your neighbor no more wrongs your dog than your car would be wronged if the windshield were smashed. Your neighbor's duties involving your dog are indirect duties to you. More generally, all of our duties regarding animals are indirect duties to one another — to humanity.

How could someone try to justify such a view? Someone might say that your dog doesn't feel anything and so isn't hurt by your neighbor's kick, doesn't care about the pain since none is felt, is as unaware of anything as is your windshield. Someone might say this, but no rational person will, since, among other considerations, such a view will commit anyone who holds it to the position that no human being feels pain either — that human beings also don't care about what happens to them. A second possibility is that though both humans and your dog are hurt when kicked, it is only human pain that matters. But, again, no rational person can believe this. Pain is pain wherever it occurs. If your neighbor's causing you pain is wrong because of the pain that is caused, we cannot rationally ignore or dismiss the moral relevance of the pain that your dog feels.

Philosophers who hold indirect duty views — and some still do — have come to understand that they must avoid the two defects just noted: that is, both the views that animals don't feel anything as well as the idea that only human pain can be morally relevant. Among such thinkers the sort of view now favored is one or other form of what is called *contractarianism*.

Here, very crudely, is the root idea: morality consists of a set of rules that individuals voluntarily agree to abide by, as we do when we sign a contract (hence the name contractarianism). Those who understand and accept the terms of the contract are covered directly; they have rights created and recognized by, and protected in, the contract. And these contractors can also have protection spelled out for others who, though they lack the ability to understand morality and so cannot sign the contract themselves, are loved or cherished by those who can. Thus young children, for example, are unable to sign contracts and lack rights. But they are protected by the contract none the less because of the sentimental interests of others, most notably their parents. So we have, then, duties involving these children, duties regarding them, but no duties to them. Our duties in their case are indirect duties to other human beings, usually their parents.

As for animals, since they cannot understand contracts, they obviously cannot sign; and since they cannot sign, they have no rights. Like children, however, some animals are the objects of the sentimental interest of others. You, for example, love your dog or cat. So those animals that enough people care about (companion animals, whales, baby seals, the American bald eagle), though they lack rights themselves, will be protected because of the sentimental interests of people. I have, then, according to contractarianism, no duty directly to your dog or any other animal, not even the duty not to cause them pain or suffering; my duty not to hurt them is a duty I have to those people who care about what happens to them. As for other animals, where no or little sentimental interest is present — in the case of farm animals, for example, or laboratory rats — what duties we have grow weaker and weaker, perhaps to the vanishing point. The pain and death they endure, though real, are not wrong if no one cares about them.

When it comes to the moral status of animals, contractarianism could be a hard view to refute if it were an adequate theoretical approach to the moral status of human beings. It is not adequate in this latter respect, however, which makes the question of its adequacy in the former case, regarding animals, utterly moot. For consider: morality, according to the (crude) contractarian position before us, consists of rules that people agree to abide by. What people? Well, enough to make a difference

— enough, that is, *collectively* to have the power to enforce the rules that are drawn up in the contract. That is very well and good for the signatories but not so good for anyone who is not asked to sign. And there is nothing in contractarianism of the sort we are discussing that guarantees or requires that everyone will have a chance to participate equally in framing the rules of morality. The result is that this approach to ethics could sanction the most blatant forms of social, economic, moral and political injustice, ranging from a repressive caste system to systematic racial or sexual discrimination. Might, according to this theory, does make right. Let those who are the victims of injustice suffer as they will. It matters not so long as no one else — no contractor, or too few of them —cares about it. Such a theory takes one's moral breath away ... as if, for example, there would be nothing wrong with apartheid in South Africa if few white South Africans were upset by it. A theory with so little to recommend it at the level of the ethics of our treatment of our fellow humans cannot have anything more to recommend it when it comes to the ethics of how we treat our fellow animals.

The version of contractarianism just examined is, as I have noted, a crude variety, and in fairness to those of a contractarian persuasion it must be noted that much more refined, subtle and ingenious varieties are possible. For example, John Rawls, in his *A Theory of Justice,* sets forth a version of contractarianism that forces contractors to ignore the accidental features of being a human being — for example, whether one is white or black, male or female, a genius or modest intellect. Only by ignoring such features, Rawls believes, can we ensure that the principles of justice that contractors would agree upon are not based on bias or prejudice. Despite the improvement a view such as Rawls's represents over the cruder forms of contractarianism, it remains deficient: it systematically denies that we have direct duties to those human beings who do not have a sense of justice — young children, for instance, and many mentally retarded humans. And yet it seems reasonably certain that, were we to torture a young child or a retarded elder, we would be doing something that wronged him or her, not something that would be wrong if (and only if) other humans with a sense of justice were upset. And since this is true in the case of these humans, we cannot rationally deny the same in the case of animals.

Indirect duty views, then, including the best among them, fail to command our rational assent. Whatever ethical theory we should accept rationally, therefore, it must at least recognize that we have some duties directly to animals, just as we have some duties directly to each other. The next two theories I'll sketch attempt to meet this requirement.

The first I call the cruelty-kindness view. Simply stated, this says that we have a direct duty to be kind to animals and a direct duty not to be cruel to them. Despite the familiar, reassuring ring of these ideas, I do not believe that this view offers an adequate theory. To make this clearer, consider kindness. A kind person acts from a certain kind of motive — compassion or concern, for example. And that is a virtue. But there is no guarantee that a kind act is a right act. If I am a generous racist, for example, I will be inclined to act kindly towards members of my own race, favoring their interests above those of others. My kindness would be real and, so far as it goes, good. But I trust it is too obvious to require argument that my kind acts may not be above moral reproach — may, in fact, be positively wrong because rooted in injustice. So kindness, notwithstanding its status as a virtue to be encouraged, simply will not carry the weight of a theory of right action.

Cruelty fares no better. People or their acts are cruel if

they display either a lack of sympathy for or, worse, the presence of enjoyment in another's suffering. Cruelty in all its guises is a bad thing, a tragic human failing. But just as a person's being motivated by kindness does not guarantee that he or she does what is right, so the absence of cruelty does not ensure that he or she avoids doing what is wrong. Many people who perform abortions, for example, are not cruel, sadistic people. But that fact alone does not settle the terrible difficult question of the morality of abortion. The case is no different when we examine the ethics of our treatment of animals. So yes, let us be for kindness and against cruelty. But let us not suppose that being for the one and against the other answers questions about moral right and wrong.

Some people think that the theory we are looking for is utilitarianism. A utilitarian accepts two moral principles. The first is that of equality: everyone's interests count, and similar interests must be counted as having similar weight or importance. White or black, American or Iranian, human or animal — everyone's pain or frustration matters, and matters just as much as the equivalent pain or frustration of anyone else. The second principle a utilitarian accepts is that of utility: do the act that will bring about the best balance between satisfaction and frustration for everyone affected by the outcome.

As a utilitarian, then, here is how I am to approach the task of deciding what I morally ought to do: I must ask who will be affected if I choose to do one thing rather than another, how much each individual will be affected, and where the best results are most likely to lie — which option, in other words, is most likely to bring about the best results, the best balance between satisfaction and frustration. That option, whatever it may be, is the one I ought to choose. That is where my moral duty lies.

The great appeal of utilitarianism rests with its

uncompromising *egalitarianism:* everyone's interests count as much as the like interests of everyone else. The kind of odious discrimination that some forms of contractarianism can justify — discrimination based on race or sex, for example — seems disallowed in principle by utilitarianism, as is speciesism, systematic discrimination based on species membership.

The equality we find in utilitarianism, however, is not the sort an advocate of animal or human rights should have in mind. Utilitarianism has no room for the equal moral rights of different individuals because it has no room for their equal inherent value or worth. What has value for the utilitarian is the satisfaction of an individual's interests, not the individual whose interests they are. A universe in which you satisfy your desire for water, food and warmth is, other things being equal, better than a universe in which these desires are frustrated. And the same is true in the case of an animal with similar desires. But neither you nor the animal have any value in your own right. Only your feelings do.

Here is an analogy to help make the philosophical point clearer: a cup contains different liquids, sometimes sweet, sometimes bitter, sometimes a mix of the two. What has value are the liquids; the sweeter the better, the bitterer the worse. The cup, the container, has no value. It is what goes into it, not what they go into, that has value. For the utilitarian you and I are like the cup: we have no value as individuals and thus no equal value. What has value is what goes into us, what we serve as receptacles for: our feelings of satisfaction have positive value, our feelings of frustration negative value.

Serious problems arise for utilitarianism when we remind ourselves that it enjoins us to bring about the best consequences. What does this mean? It doesn't mean the best consequences for me alone, or for my family or friends, or any other person taken individually. No, what we must do is, roughly, as follows: we must add up (somehow!) the separate satisfactions and frustrations of everyone likely to be affected by our choice, the satisfactions in one column, the frustrations in the other. We must total each column for each of the options before us. That is what it means to say the theory is aggregative. And then we must choose that option which is most likely to bring about the best balance of totalled satisfactions over totalled frustrations. Whatever act would lead to this outcome is the one we ought morally to perform — it is where our moral duty lies. And that act quite clearly might not be the same one that would bring about the best results for me personally, or for my family or friends, or for a lab animal. The best aggregated consequences for everyone concerned are not necessarily the best for each individual.

That utilitarianism is an aggregative theory — different individuals' satisfactions or frustrations are added, or summed, or totalled — is the key objection to this theory. My Aunt Bea is old, inactive, a cranky, sour person, though not physically ill. She prefers to go on living. She is also rather rich. I could make a fortune if I could get my hands on her money, money she intends to give me in any event, after she dies, but which she refuses to give me now. In order to avoid a huge tax bite, I plan to donate a handsome sum of my profits to a local children's hospital. Many, many children will benefit from my generosity, and much joy will be brought to their parents, relatives and friends. If I don't get the money rather soon, all these ambitions will come to naught. The once-in-a-lifetime opportunity to make a real killing will be gone. Why, then, not kill my Aunt Bea? Oh, of course I *might* get caught. But I'm no fool and, besides, her doctor can be counted on to cooperate (he has an eye for the same investment and I happen to know a good deal about his shady past). The deed can be done...professionally, shall we say. there is *very* little chance of getting caught. And as for my conscience being guilt-ridden, I am a resourceful sort of fellow and will take more than sufficient comfort —as I lie on the beach at Acapulco — in contemplating the joys and health I have brought to so many others.

Suppose Aunt Bea is killed and the rest of the story comes out as told. Would I have done anything wrong? Anything immoral? One would have thought that I had. Not according to utilitarianism. Since what I have done has brought about the best balance between total satisfaction and frustration for all those affected by the outcome, my action is not wrong. Indeed, in killing Aunt Bea the physician and I did what duty required.

This same kind of argument can be repeated in all sorts of cases, illustrating, time after time, how the utilitarian's position leads to results that impartial people find morally callous. It *is* wrong to kill my Aunt Bea in the name of bringing about the best results for others. A good end does not justify an evil means. Any adequate moral theory will have to explain why this is so. Utilitarianism fails in this respect and so cannot be the theory we seek.

What to do? Where to begin anew? The place to begin, I think, is with the utilitarian's view of the value of the individual — or, rather, lack of value. In its place, suppose we consider that you and I, for example, do have value as individuals — what we'll call *inherent value.* To say we have such value is to say that we are something more than, something different from, mere receptacles. Moreover, to ensure that we do not pave the way for such injustices as slavery or sexual discrimination, we must believe that all who have inherent value have it equally, regardless of their sex, race, religion, birthplace and so on. Similarly to be discarded as irrelevant are one's talents or skills, intelligence and wealth, personality or pathology, whether one is loved and admired or despised and loathed. The genius and the retarded child, the prince and the pauper, the brain surgeon and the fruit vendor, Mother Teresa and the most unscrupulous used-car salesman — all have inherent value, all possess it equally, and have an equal right to be treated with respect, to be treated in ways that do not reduce them to the status of things, as if they existed as resources for others. My value as an individual is independent of my usefulness to you. Yours is not dependent on your usefulness to me. For either of us to treat the other in ways that fail to show respect for the other's independent value is to act immorally, to violate the individual's rights.

Some of the rational virtues of this view — what I call the rights view — should be evident. Unlike (crude) contractarianism, for example, the rights view in *principle* denies the moral tolerability of any and all forms of racial, sexual or social discrimination; and unlike utilitarianism, this view *in principle* denies that we can justify good results by using evil means that violate an individual's rights — denies, for example, that it could be moral to kill my Aunt Bea to harvest beneficial consequences for others. That would be to sanction the disrespectful treatment of the individual in the name of the social good, something the rights view will not — categorically will not — ever allow.

The rights view, I believe, is rationally the most satisfactory moral theory. It surpasses all other theories in the degree to which it illuminates and explains the foundations of our duties to one another — the domain of human morality. On this score it has the best reasons, the best arguments, on its side. Of course, if it were possible to show that only human beings are included within its scope, then a person like myself, who believes in animal rights, would be obliged to look elsewhere.

But attempts to limit its scope to humans only can be shown to be rationally defective. Animals, it is true, lack many of the abilities humans possess. They can't read, do higher mathematics, build a bookcase or make *baba ghanoush*. Neither can many human beings, however, and yet we don't (and shouldn't) say that they (these humans) therefore have less inherent value, less of a right to be treated with respect, than do others. It is the *similarities* between those human beings who most clearly, most non-controversially have such value (the people reading this, for example), not our differences, that matter most. And the really crucial, the basic similarity is simply this: we are each of us the experiencing subject of a life, a conscious creature having an individual welfare that has importance to us whatever our usefulness to others. We want and prefer things, believe and feel things, recall and expect things. And all these dimensions of our life, including our pleasure and pain, our enjoyment and suffering, our satisfaction and frustration, our continued existence or our untimely death — all make a difference to the quality of our life as lived, as experienced, by us as individuals. As the same is true of those animals that concern us (the ones that are eaten and trapped, for example), they too must be viewed as the experiencing subjects of a life, with inherent value of their own.

Some there are who resist the idea that animals have inherent value. 'Only humans have such value,' they profess. How might this narrow view be defended? Shall we say that only humans have the requisite intelligence, or autonomy, of reason? But there are many, many humans who fail to meet these standards and yet are reasonably viewed as having value above and beyond their usefulness to others. Shall we claim that only humans belong to the right species, the species *Homo sapiens?* But this is blatant speciesism. Will it be said, then, that all — and only — humans have immortal souls? Then our opponents have their work cut out for them. I am myself not ill-disposed to the proposition that there are immortal souls. Personally, I profoundly hope I have one.

But I would not want to rest my position on a controversial ethical issue on the even more controversial question about who or what has an immortal soul. That is to dig one's hole deeper, not to climb out. Rationally, it is better to resolve moral issues without making more controversial assumptions than are needed. The question of who has inherent value is such a question, one that is resolved more rationally without the introduction of the idea of immortal souls than by its use.

Well, perhaps some will say that animals have some inherent value, only less than we have. Once again, however, attempts to defend this view can be shown to lack rational justification. What could be the basis of our having more inherent value than animals? Their lack of reason, or autonomy, or intellect? Only if we are willing to make the same judgement in the case of humans who are similarly deficient. But it is not true that such humans —the retarded child, for example, or the mentally deranged — have less inherent value than you or I. Neither, then, can we rationally sustain the view that animals like them in being the experiencing subjects of a life have less inherent value. *All* who have inherent value have it *equally,* whether they be human animals or not.

Inherent value, then, belongs equally to those who are the experiencing subjects of a life. Whether it belongs to others — to rocks and rivers, trees and glaciers, for example — we do not know and may never know. But neither do we need to know, if we are to make the case for animal rights. We do not need to know, for example, how many people are eligible to vote in the next presidential election before we can know whether I am. Similarly, we do not need to know how many individuals have inherent value before we can know that some do. When it comes to the case for animal rights, then, what we need to know is whether the animals that, in our culture, are routinely eaten, hunted and used in our laboratories, for example, are like us in being subjects of a life. And we do know this. We do know that many — literally, billions and billions —of these animals are the subjects of a life in the sense explained and so have inherent value if we do. And since, in order to arrive at the best theory of our duties to one another, we must recognize our equal inherent value as individuals, reason — not sentiment, not emotion — reason compels us to recognize the equal inherent value of these animals and, with this, their equal right to be treated with respect.

That, *very* roughly, is the shape and feel of the case for animal rights. Most of the details of the supporting argument are missing. They are to be found in the book to which I alluded earlier. Here, the details go begging, and I must, in closing, limit myself to four final points.

The first is how the theory that underlies the case for animal rights shows that the animal rights movement is a part of, not antagonistic to, the human rights movement. The theory that rationally grounds the rights of animals also grounds the rights of humans. Thus those involved in the animal rights movement are partners in the struggle to secure respect for human rights — the rights of women, for example, or minorities, or workers. The animal rights movement is cut from the same moral cloth as these.

Second, having set out the broad outlines of the rights view, I can now say why its implications for farming and science, among other fields, are both clear and uncompromising. In the case of the use of animals in science, the rights view is categorically abolitionist. Lab animals are not our tasters; we are not their kings. Because these animals are treated routinely, systematically as if their value were reducible to their usefulness to others, they are routinely, systematically treated with a lack of respect, and thus are their rights routinely, systematically violated. This is just as true when they are used in trivial, duplicative, unnecessary or unwise research as it is when they are used in studies that hold out real promise of human benefits. We can't justify harming or killing a human being (my Aunt Bea, for example) just for these sorts of reason. Neither can we do so even in the case of so "lowly" a creature as a laboratory rat. It is not just refinement or reduction that is called for, not just larger, cleaner cages, not just more generous use of anesthetic or the elimination of multiple surgery, not just tidying up the system. It is complete replacement. The best we can do when it comes to using animals in science is — not to use them. That is where our duty lies, according to the rights view.

As for commercial animal agriculture, the rights view takes a similar abolitionist position. The fundamental moral wrong here is not that animals are kept in stressful close confinement or in isolation, or that their pain and suffering, their needs and preferences are ignored or discounted. All these *are* wrong, of course, but they are not the fundamental wrong. They are symptoms and effects of the deeper, systematic wrong that allows these animals to be viewed and treated as lacking independent value, as resources for us — as, indeed, a renewable resource. Giving farm animals more space, more natural environments, more companions does not right the fundamental wrong, any more than giving lab animals more anesthesia or bigger, cleaner cages would right the fundamental wrong in their case. Nothing less than the total dissolution of commercial animal agriculture will do this, just as, for similar reasons I won't develop at length here, morality requires nothing less than the total elimination of hunting and trapping for commercial and sporting ends. The rights view's implications, then, as I have said, are clear and uncompromising.

My last two points are about philosophy, my profession. It is, most obviously, no substitute for political action. The words I have written here and in other places by themselves don't change a thing. It is what we do with the thoughts that the words express — our acts, our deeds — that changes things. All that philoshopy can do, and all I have attempted, is to offer a vision of what our deeds should aim at. And the why. But not the how.

Finally, I am reminded of my thoughtful critic, the one I mentioned earlier, who chastised me for being too cerebral. Well, cerebral I have been: indirect duty views, utilitarianism, contractarianism — hardly the stuff deep passions are made of. I am also reminded, however, of the image another friend once set before me — the image of the ballerina as expressive of disciplined passion. Long hours of sweat and toil, of loneliness and practice, of doubt and fatigue: those are the discipline of her craft. But the passion is there too, the fierce drive to excel, to speak through her body, to do it right, to pierce our minds. That is the image of philosophy I would leave with you, not 'too cerebral' but *disciplined passion.* Of the discipline enough has been seen. As for the passion: there are times, and these not infrequent, when tears come to my eyes when I see, or read, or hear of the wretched plight of animals in the hands of humans. Their pain, their suffering, their loneliness, their innocence, their death. Anger. Rage. Pity. Sorrow. Disgust. The whole creation groans under the weight of the evil we humans visit upon these mute, powerless creatures. It *is* our hearts, not just our heads, that call for an end to it all, that demand of us that we overcome, for them, the habits and forces behind their systematic oppression. All great movements, it is written, go through three stages: ridicule, discussion, adoption. It is the realization of this third stage, adoption, that requires both our passion and our discipline, our hearts and our heads. The fate of animals is in our hands. God grant we are equal to the task.

3

But for the Sake of Some Little Mouthful of Flesh

I first became involved in the struggle for animal rights because I became convinced that eating animals (or, as people in the western world say, "eating meat") is not morally defensible. That was back in the early seventies. The beginnings of my odyssey back then owe a great deal to the influence Gandhi had on my thinking. The reasons I have for not eating animals have changed somewhat in the intervening years, but not my resolve to abstain from eating them. In fact, I no longer have to struggle with myself over this issue. I no longer have the slightest temptation to eat the flesh of a once living and breathing creature. Just the opposite. Today I find it remarkable that most of the people I know, and certainly most of the people in the western world, not only experience this temptation but daily give in to it. How is it possible, I wonder, for otherwise decent people to engage in a practice that is so patently, so demonstrably immoral?

I try to be understanding and patient with my meat-eating friends. After all, I myself once ate animals and didn't think a thing of it. More than this, I was once a butcher's apprentice and actually might have become a butcher but for a series of contingencies over which I exercised no clearly discernible control. Nevertheless, the moral case against eating animals is so overwhelming, so much on the side of reason, that it really does take my breath away when I see otherwise informed, ostensibly ethical people devour a chicken leg or go bonkers over a steak. Morally speaking, I feel like throwing up.

I don't think there is any easy way to lead people to a more respectful diet. There isn't some simple incantation or algebraic formula, no mystical mantra or aerobic exercise, that will change people overnight. All that there is, is calm, cool, informed reflection. All that there is, one might say, is the voice of reason. But that voice, though not impotent by any means, more than has its work cut out for it in the present case, speaking out, as it must, against the enormously powerful forces of social custom and personal habit. Here, surely, animal rights is David and the vast wrong of meat eating is Goliath.

In my philosophical writings, most notably *The Case for Animal Rights,* I have attempted to articulate and defend the deep intellectual basis against eating animals. In the essay that follows I take a less demanding but equally germane view. I try to address ordinary meat-eaters where they are, not where the force of a sophisticated moral logic wants them to be. All that I ask is that people who eat animals stop for a moment to think about the implications of what they are doing — for themselves, for other human beings, and for the nonhuman animals who are fried, broiled, roasted, fricasseed, and in other ways "prepared" to satisfy the demands of the human palate.

For those who refuse even to think a moment about this, there is, of course, no argument that can possibly dissuade them. These people must be given up as morally lost, at least for the present. For those of us involved in the struggle for animal rights, the people we want to encounter and (*politely!*) challenge are those who *will* think a moment about what they are doing, who they are, and what they are making of their lives. In these people lies the future growth and strength of the Animal Rights Movement. I only hope that some of these people will read what I have written and find it useful in their quest for personal fulfillment.

Most people like animals. Cats and dogs are favorites. But the good feelings many people have for whales and dolphins, baby seals and elephants show that even wild animals can come within the mantle of our affections. Animals don't have to live with us to be liked by us.

Children reveal how generous we are in our natural love of animals. Any grade school teacher knows that nothing gets the attention of youngsters like a class visit by an animal, whatever the species. Children's bedrooms are veritable menageries of stuffed creatures, and the stories young people eagerly read, listen to, or watch are as much about the travails of bears and rabbits as they are about the adventures of human beings. Even adults find it natural to drive cars named Mustang, Lynx, and Cougar, or to root for athletic teams called the Colts, Rams, or Cardinals. Some of the habits of childhood remain for a lifetime.

One of these habits concerns food. Most people who live in the western world are taught to eat meat from infancy onward. And most people who acquire this habit never give it up. Perhaps some never stop to think about it. But whether thought about or not, we face a strange paradox: On the one hand, people naturally love animals; on the other, they eat them. How is it possible to eat what one loves?

One possible answer is that people do not love the

animals they eat or eat the animals they love. And it is true that comparatively few Westerners feel much affection for domesticated "food animals," as they are called —cows, pigs, chickens and turkeys, for example. Why these animals tend not to be loved by us, while others are, poses many interesting questions. We in the West are shocked to learn that Koreans and other Asians *eat dog.* And yet Hindus are no less aghast that Westerners *eat cow,* and many other people from various parts of the world wonder how humans can eat *any* animal. Love is fickle, it seems, even in the case of our love for animals. It is difficult to understand how some people can adamantly refuse to eat cats and dogs because they love them, and then turn around and gladly eat other animals who are not essentially different. Cows and pigs, for example, just like dogs and cats, see and hear, are hungry and thirsty, feel pain and pleasure, like companionship and warmth. If we do not eat the latter, how can it be fair or rational to eat the former?

Perhaps part of the answer lies in the fact that people do not have to kill the animals they eat. Other people do this for them. So perhaps the ancient adage, "Out of sight, out of mind," applies. Because we do not see animals die, perhaps we can pretend they are not killed. By not being a party to their slaughter people can have a psychological shield that protects them from seeing steaks and chops as parts of dead animals — as pieces of corpses. Certainly many people would give up eating meat if they had to slaughter animals themselves. The emotional trauma would be too great.

These psychological defenses may not be strong enough. How would we fare psychologically if the walls of slaughterhouses were made of glass? What would we feel and do if we *saw* the death of so-called "food animals"? Might not the psychological shield break if people peered through these glass walls and saw the meat on their plate for what it really is, not for what they pretend it to be?

But slaughterhouses do not have glass walls. And few people ever venture inside. And why should they? Whatever the details, everybody understands without looking that they can't be pretty. So why go in? Who wants or needs to see all the blood and gore?

Most people are satisfied with this response, at least until they begin to think about it. After all, we force ourselves to look at many things that aren't "pretty" —the mass graves of innocent women and children massacred in Vietnam, for example, and the merciless exploitation of Jews at the hands of Nazis. We do not want to look, of course, and we do not enjoy what we see. Yet we understand the need to confront the truth, however ugly it may be, lest we forget. We owe the victims of large-scale human evil at least this much.

Do we owe less to the animals slaughtered for food? Certainly the statistics are staggering: Over 5 *billion* slaughtered annually, just in the United States, approximately 4,000 killed every second of every day. In terms of sheer numbers even the worst human atrocities are dwarfed by comparison. Of these atrocities we understand the need to remind ourselves. In the face of animal slaughter we look away. How can it be right to force ourselves to confront the one and allow ourselves to avoid the other?

For many people the explanation is simple: Despite the natural affection we humans have for some animals, it is *not wrong* to kill them for food. Of course these people don't like the idea of animals being slaughtered and would not (or could not) perform the slaughter themselves. But while it is wrong to kill human beings for food, for example, it is not wrong in their view to do this to animals.

How can this be? How is it possible for the one to be wrong and the other not? Some reason must be given. Many have been. One relies on religious beliefs about the soul. Many people think killing is wrong only when the victim has an immortal soul. And this belief, coupled with the additional belief that only human beings possess immortal souls, does offer a reason which, if true, could justify killing animals for food.

How adequate is this response? Different people dispute it for different reasons. Some dispute it because they believe that *nothing* has an immortal soul. Others dispute it because they believe that *everything* does. Who (or what) has an immortal soul, in short, is a controversial question. But whatever the answer offered it proves to be irrelevant. For *how long* individuals live makes no difference to how they should be treated while alive. If a dog has been hit by a car and we can alleviate her pain, then it is wrong not to do so. It would be morally grotesque to say that we need not help "because she will not live forever." It would be no less grotesque to suppose that we might justify killing "soul-less" animals "because they have no life beyond the grave." If anything, just the opposite would be true. For if animals have no prospect of a life *after* this one, then we should do everything we can to insure that the life they do have — *this* one — is as long and full as possible. This we hardly do by slaughtering them at the rate of almost 14 million a day — just in the United States. Rather than this defense of slaughtering "food animals" serving to justify what goes on in slaughterhouses, it actually demands that we close them.

A second response also relies on religious beliefs. "The Holy Bible reveals that God has given us dominion over animals," it is said. "This means we are entitled to do to animals whatever is necessary to promote our interests or satisfy our needs, including slaughtering them for food." As was true of the previous response, this one encounters dissenting voices — for example, the voices of atheists, who deny that there is a God to tell us anything, and the voices of followers of religions other than Judaism and Christianity, who do not accept the Holy Bible as God's Word. But one can counter this response without abandoning the Judeo-Christian basis on which it stands. For 'dominion' in the Biblical context clearly does not mean 'tyranny'; it means 'stewardship'. God enjoins us to be as caring and compassionate in our relationship with His creation as He is in His relationship with us. Like Him, we are to be "Good Shepherds."

Are we? No one can attempt to answer this question and ignore what goes on in slaughterhouses. For it is there that we see most vividly what our God-like stewardship comes to in the end. It is scarcely believable that anyone could hope that God will someday *treat us* in the way "food animals" are treated by the slaughterer. Who could possibly look forward with joyful longing to the prospect of meeting *this* sort of deity "face to face"? The influential Anglican cleric William Ralph Inge (Dean Inge) writes insightfully when he observes that "we have enslaved the rest of the animal creation... so badly that beyond doubt, if they were to formulate a religion, they would depict the Devil in human form." The massive scale of animal slaughter for food more than confirms our failure to live up to our role of "good shepherd."

"Even so," it may be said, "it is undeniably true that God did give us animals to eat. And since we can hardly eat them without slaughtering them, He cannot look with disfavor on our killing them either — provided, of course, we do so humanely." This response overlooks too much and accepts too little. It overlooks the fact that, judged in Biblical terms, the original diet given to human beings clearly was vegetarian. As *Genesis* 1:29 declares, "And God said, Behold, I have given you every herb bearing seed, which is upon the face of all the earth, and every tree, in which is the fruit of a tree yielding seed: to you it shall be for meat." *That* was humankind's diet "in the beginning."

The current response also accepts too little because it is satisfied with the spiritual status quo. *Genesis* reveals how things once were and should have remained. In the Biblical account we find that it was only after humans disobeyed God and were expelled from Eden — indeed, only after the Flood — that God gave us the choice to eat animals. To act on that choice thus is a sign of our disappointment of God's original hopes for us, whereas to refuse to eat animals is, in Leo Tolstoy's words, "the first step" in our journey back to a proper, loving relationship with God and His creation. "The Vegetarian movement," Tolstoy writes, "ought to fill with gladness the souls of those who have at heart the realization of God's kingdom upon earth... because (the decision not to eat animals) serves as a criterion by which we know that the pursuit of moral perfection on the part of man is genuine and sincere." People who defend eating meat and slaughtering animals "because of what the Bible says" thus are somewhat confused. It is a graceless religious faith, one grown fat and sloppy from lack of spiritual exercise, that happily accepts humanity's permanent alienation from God. One would perhaps do better to have no religious faith at all.

Whatever one's religious beliefs, each of us can agree on a number of plain facts. Humans belong to one biological species (Homo sapiens); all other animals belong to other biological species. Perhaps it will be suggested that this is why killing humans is, while killing "food animals" is not, wrong.

No thoughtful person will accept this response. As a piece of logic it is indistinguishable from defenses of the worst human prejudices. Consider the racist: "Only members of my race really count; people who belong to other races aren't our equals." And the sexist: "Only members of my sex really count; others really aren't our equals." Both prejudices rest on the same error. Both take some biological fact (one's race or sex) and make that fact the basis of moral preeminence. But no members of a given race are better than others *just because they belong to that race,* and no members of a given sex are better *just because of the sex they are.* Biological facts (race and sex, for example) are not the foundation of morality.

This is no less true of species membership than of other kinds of biological classification. We humans are not morally preeminent just because we belong to the species *Homo sapiens.* People who believe that we are preeminent for this reason are called "speciesists." Speciesists purvey as much truth as racists and sexists. A speciesist can justify slaughtering animals at least as much as a white racist can justify lynching blacks.

Biological considerations about species membership are not the only allegedly "scientific fact" put forward to defend slaughtering animals for food. The French philosopher René Descartes teaches that nonhuman animals lack consciousness, not a little but a lot. Hogs, ckickens and cows, cats, dogs and dolphins — every nonhuman animal is totally lacking in conscious awareness in his view. Some people who today profess to have a "scientific understanding of the world" continue to accept Descartes teachings. For these people a chicken and a hog are fundamentally like an ear of corn and an eggplant: Like vegetables, animals have no mind. Since neither is aware of anything, neither feels any pain. And since both lack consciousness completely, death does not cancel any of their future experiences. For these scientists it is not more wrong to slaughter an animal than it is to pick a radish or harvest a potato. In the case of human beings, however, Cartesian scientists, because they see the presence of mind, also see the evil of death. It *is* wrong to kill humans for food; it is *not* wrong to kill nonhuman animals for this reason.

Cartesianism is so much at odds with common sense

that most Cartesians are of the "closet" variety: They keep it to themselves. But there *are* Cartesians out there, and not a few can be found in commercial animal agriculture. They think people who care about animals are dumb and emotional, not, like Cartesians, smart and scientific. In displaying these attitudes present-day Cartesians continue to keep alive the attitudes of Descartes himself. "My opinion," he writes, "is not so much cruel to animals as it is indulgent to men — at least those who are not given to the superstitions of Pythagoras — since it absolves them of the suspicion of crime when they kill or eat animals." Pythagoras, it is perhaps unnecessary to note, was a vegetarian.

Descartes denies a mind (consciousness) to nonhuman animals because he thinks they are unable to use language. Critics have pointed out that the same is true of many human beings and that some animals, contrary to Descartes's denial, *can* use a language (for example, some chimpanzees have been taught American Sign Language for the Deaf).

Both objections have a place. But neither gets to the crux of the matter. That concerns the Cartesian view that individuals lack consciousness if they lack the ability to use a language. There are overwhelmingly good reasons against this assumption. To see what they are, consider the following.

Human children don't come into the world knowing how to talk; they have to be taught. Unless they contribute something to the learning process, however, they will never learn. If we say 'ball' to a child and the child does not hear, or does not see, or does not understand what we are referring to, or does not remember what we said a moment ago — if the child is deficient in these ways, no instruction can take place. We can say 'ball' till we exhaust ourselves and the child won't learn a thing. Human children, in other words, must be conscious, must be aware of things, *before* they learn to use a language. If they were not, they could never learn to use one. And this means that children must have *pre*-verbal and, so *non*-linguistic awareness. In some way (which may remain forever mysterious to us) young children are able to represent the world to themselves without using words.

This finding destroys any plausible "scientific" basis for Cartesianism. It must be rank prejudice, not respect for science, that would attribute non-linguistic awareness to human children, on the one hand, and deny this in the case of nonhuman animals, on the other. If the former can be aware of things without knowing how to use a language, the same can be true of the latter. There is no good reason to deny a mind (consciousness) to hogs, cows, chickens and other "food animals."

In fact, of course, there are very good reasons to affirm the presence of mental awareness in their case. The central nervous system of these animals resembles that of human beings in fundamentally important ways. It is not as though we humans have brains, for example, while chickens and veal calves have empty heads. The behavior of these animals, moreover, resembles human behavior in many instances, including, for example, aversion to pain and the expression of preferences, and the display of feelings such as anger and boredom. By way of illustration: Piglets not only suckle at the teats of their mother; they *enjoy* doing so. And adult sows rather *dislike* being severely confined; they are *frustrated* when tethered, sometimes to the point of chronic depression. Will those who profess to respect "science" judge otherwise? Then they must swallow Voltaire's barbed wit. "Has nature arranged all the means of feeling in this animal," he asks, "so that it may not feel?" Against those who profess to understand the world from a "scientific point of view" Voltaire has the last word: "Do not suppose this impertinent contradiction in nature."

"But Man is the only *rational* animal," it may be said. This is both false and irrelevant. It is false because many animals, including so-called "food animals", display their capacity to reason by their ability to learn. And it is in any event irrelevant since the ability to reason is not a decisive consideration in determining the wrongness of killing. If it were we would be at liberty to kill a human being who, for one reason or another, lacks this ability: infants of a few days or a few months of age, the insane, the senile. But not even those most anxious to exploit "food animals" would go so far as to suggest that these humans may be killed with impunity. *Or so we must hope.* Once again, therefore, it can only be a blatant double standard that would forbid the killing of these humans but allow the killing of these animals.

So-called "food animals", then, are not on all fours with heads of lettuce and stalks of celery. Like these vegetables, it is true, these animals are alive. But like us, and in this respect unlike all vegetables, they *live their life.* They are *somebody,* not some thing. Their death marks the end of a biographical, not merely a biological, life. To kill them inhumanely is of course to cause them gratuitous pain. And that is gratuitously immoral. But to kill them at all is to cancel their psychological sojourn on this earth. It is to nullify *their* future, depriving them of those experiences that would have been theirs but for the hand of Man. In certain fundamental respects — though not, of course, in all respects — "food animals" are like human beings. Both are selves with beliefs, preferences, desires and social needs, not just bodies with hearts and lungs. As Charles Darwin noted more than a hundred years ago, the mental life of these animals differs from ours in degrees, not in kind.

This insight into the nature of "food animals" presses the ethical question of their slaughter home with additional force. How can it be moral to kill one self so that others might benefit? In the case of human ethics we recognize a very limited range of circumstances in which killing may be justified. When it comes to self-defense or on grounds of mercy, many people believe we are morally justified in killing another human being. But no one will seriously maintain that some human beings are entitled to kill other humans just because members of the former group stand to gain something as a result. Nazis may have thought this of Jews, and members of the Ku Klux Klan may think this of blacks. But otherwise sane and sensible people will abhor such an ethic.

And yet it is this same pattern of discrimination that allows us to tolerate (and, in the case of many, to support) the slaughter of more than a half-million animals every hour of every day — just in the United States. It is ludicrous to suggest that beef cattle and broiler chickens are *threatening our life* and so may be killed in the name of self-defense. No less preposterous is the suggestion that these animals must have their throats slit *in the name of mercy.* No, the only plausible reason why people tolerate or support this carnage is because they see animals as *other* than they are. Animals are "them." Humans are "us." And the standards of decency that apply between "us" just don't extend to the treatment of "them."

So many will say. But so, too, says the moral racist who withholds equal moral consideration from those who belong to the "inferior races." And so, too, says the sexist who denies equal moral consideration to those who belong to "the inferior sex." Those people who do not see the moral ties that bind humans to animals suffer from the same kind of moral blindness. *Of course* they do not see animals as "us." *Of course* they see animals as "them." In these false perceptions lies the very blindness from which they suffer. Only, of course, it is the animals who really suffer. And on a massive scale. Do we dare to speak of a *Holocaust for the animals?* May we depict the horror they must endure, using this fearful image of wanton inhumanity, without desecrating the memory of those innocents who died in the death camps?

The Pulitzer Prize winning novelist Isaac Bashevis Singer thinks we may. And must. Himself a Jew and a vegetarian (having changed his diet for ethical reasons late in life), Singer returns to this theme again and again in his fiction. As the character Herman says in one of his stories, most humans think that "all other creatures were created merely to provide (us) with food, pelts, to be tormented, exterminated. In relation to (animals), all people are Nazis." Knowing Singer as we do, we also know that Herman speaks for him when, full of despair, he concludes that "for the animals it is an eternal Treblinka."

This last point highlights the shallowness of most of the moral debate about animal slaughter. That debate centers on which method of slaughter is the most "humane." Presumably this would be the method that causes the least amount of pain and distress, both before and during slaughter. How are we to decide this is far from clear, but the protracted controversy over the comparative "humaneness" of kosher and nonkosher slaughter, for example, more than confirms the suspicion that this is an issue quite capable of having a life of its own.

Important though it undeniably is, the question about the "humaneness" of alternative methods of slaughter is not the fundamental moral issue. That issue concerns *not how we do but whether we should* slaughter animals for food. And that issue is not answered in the least by comparing the alleged pain indices of various methods.

The basic moral issue, then, is simply this: What justifies us in ending the biographical life of sentient, social, intelligent creatures so that we might eat them? It cannot be because we have souls and they do not. Nor because we have "dominion" over them. Nor because God allows us to eat them. Nor because we have a mind and they lack one. Nor because we are rational and they are not. Each and every one of these attempted defenses collapses under the weight of careful thought. Where, then, is the rational basis for a practice which, just in the United States, bleeds the life out of some 500,000 animals in the time it takes to read this essay?

"We *must* eat meat!" may be the reply. "If we didn't we couldn't live a long and healthy life ourselves. That's what makes the sacrifice of animals necessary." This response is mistaken on every possible account. Meat is not necessary for human health. Every essential nutrient obtained by eating meat and animal products can be obtained by eating a wholly non-animal diet. And as for health and longevity: all the available evidence (at least all the evidence impartially arrived at) points unambiguously to the conclusion that eating meat and animal products is potentially very bad for human health. Why? The reasons are many. Just two examples will have to suffice.

Most commercial animal farmers today practice what are called "intensive rearing" or "close confinement" methods. The animals are kept permanently indoors in conditions that severely limit their opportunities to move. Bodily motion, after all, burns calories, and calories burnt means pounds lost. (Every erstwhile dieter knows that.) Since the farmer has a strong economic interest in bringing the animals to market with as little investment as possible, it makes economic sense (or so many believe) to minimize the animals' opportunities for physical activity.

But a potential health problem demands the farmer's attention. In these crowded conditions a contagious disease could spread like wildfire through the flocks or herd. The financial loss would be very large. What to do? The favored solution is to add powerful antibiotics (penicillin and tetracycline are the most widely used) to animal feed.

The idea is to prevent diseases from breaking out rather than to attempt to cure them after they have.

What becomes of an antibiotic after animals consume it? Most is excreted in the animals' urine and feces. But not all. Varying amounts remain in the animals' bodies, stored in tissues and organs. When, after slaughter, human consumers eat the flesh of these animals, they can inadvertently take small doses of antibiotics. The results are predictable. By consuming small amounts of these drugs over a long period of time people build up immunities to them. Not surprisingly "wonder drugs" of only a few decades ago increasingly are ineffective in treating serious diseases among the human population.

But the results are even worse than this. Bacteria that thrive in the bodies of animals are beginning to show up in new, virulent strains *in the bodies of human beings*. These strains have adapted to their antibiotic enemies in the drug-war being waged by today's animal farmer; they have "learned to survive" and are no longer controllable using existing drugs. There are documented cases of people dying from bacterial diseases traceable to new strains of old diseases originating in "food animals." The National Resources Defense Council estimates that 100 to 300 fatalities and 270,000 non-fatal cases of salmonella poisoning may occur in humans because of antibiotics in animal feed. These are per year estimates for the United States. The situation likely is no better in other parts of the world. The meat people eat clearly includes more than meets the eye. Perhaps there is more than a little wisdom behind the suggestion that we change the name "Meat Counter" to "Drug Counter."

A different but no less serious problem concerns the relationship between diet and general health. People whose food habits center on meat consumption have a diet high in fat and low in carbohydrates, and a diet of this sort has been linked to the major causes of death and serious illness in the human population: various cancers (of the colon and breast, for example) and coronary diseases (heart attack, stroke, and hardening of the arteries, for instance). A vegetarian diet, by contrast, is high in carbohydrates and low in fat, and this dietary way of life has been shown to be far healthier than a diet inspired by meat consumption. It is plainly (and sometimes fatally) false that meat is necessary for "a long and healthy life", a lesson more and more health-conscious consumers are learning every day. People don't have to be motivated by respect for the rights of animals to decide not to eat them.

The remaining defenses of animal slaughter are even less palatable than those that have gone before. "Meat tastes good" is one. This settles nothing, either from the point of view of health or that of morality. If "tastes good" was the measure of what is conducive to good health many people would never liberate themselves from the candy counter (and not a few would drink and smoke themselves to death in pursuit of physical fitness). To suppose that "tastes good" is an adequate standard of *morality* is even more bizarre. One can only imagine how convenient this standard would have been to the cannibals encountered by past explorers. Perhaps that standard would have obligated these explorers to volunteer their tender bodies for the tribal stew. "It tastes good" is no more a reasonable standard of morality than is "It jumps high" or "It runs fast."

"Eating meat is convenient." "Eating meat is an American custom." "Eating meat helps me socially." "People who don't eat meat are thought to be odd." These defenses of the slaughter and consumption of animals are houses of cards. None seriously addresses the basic moral issue. None offers an even remotely adequate reason for ending the biographical life of any animal, human or otherwise. "But for the sake of some little mouthful of flesh," the Greek historian Plutarch wrote almost two thousand years ago, we deprive an animal "of the sun and light, and of that proportion of life and time it had been born into the world to enjoy." For reasons of convenience, yes. For reasons of compassion, no. Perhaps Leonardo da Vinci is right when he predicts that "the time will come when men such as I will look upon the murder of animals as they now look upon the murder of men." One can only hope that time is soon.

When the dust of the debate settles, then, one thing is abundantly clear: The arguments against the ethics of animal slaughter win the battle of ideas hands down. The standard defenses of slaughtering animals for food are deficient. And always have been. Why, then, do so many people continue to support the slaughter of animals by buying and eating meat? The simple answer is, "Because we do not always act according to the best reasons." That is both notoriously — and regrettably — true. There are many forces in addition to reason that lead us to act as we do. Anger. Pride. Jealousy. Greed. Prejudice. Contempt. Habit. Ignorance. These and countless other factors play important roles in motivating human behavior. Reason more than has its hands full in trying to cope with the demands of such a motley crew of powerful forces. No refutation of the possible defenses of animal slaughter is itself sufficient to insure that reason *will* prevail and that people *will* stop supporting the slaughter of animals.

What such a survey can show is that *if* reason prevails, *then* people will stop doing this. For there is more than food on our plates. With every meal we consume something of the substance of our own values and commit-ments. Do we respect the demands of reason? Do we value our ability to think and act on our own? Are we satisfied that we are doing the best we can with our lives? These are the truths we consume everyday, whether we eat with friends or alone.

But this review of the standard defenses of animal slaughter yields at least one other insight. Once we recognize how poor are the reasons for killing "food animals", we glimpse the deeper explanation of why so few people actually visit slaughterhouses — and why so many want to remain blissfully ignorant of what transpires there. Every thoughtful person understands the truth of Emerson's observation: "You have just dined, and however scrupulously the slaughterhouse is concealed in the graceful distance of miles, there is complicity." That sense of our own complicity is what, deep down, we hope to shield from ourselves by refusing to look the death of animals in the eye. Before any rational reflection begins we understand that, if we looked, we would see the animals' blood on our own hands. We would be aghast at ourselves for what we have done. And for what we are doing. So we look, not inside but aside, in search of every excuse not to face our involvement in the needless massacre (for that is what it is) of millions upon millions of animals, day in and day out. Opaque walls make good neighbors.

4

Animals Are Not Our Tasters; We Are Not Their Kings

Not so very long ago kings and members of the royal family had a handy way to discover whether an ambitious rival had poisoned their food. Some powerless serf was forced to sample the meal. If he experienced no ill effects, then the food was judged suitable for the king. If the taster became ill or died, then the food never touched royal lips. The fact that the taster sometimes became sick or died carried no moral weight. The important thing was to protect those in power, not worry about the rights of those lacking royal blood.

Today, of course, we decry — at least with words — the idea that one human being could be so ruthlessly exploited in the name of protecting the interests of others. The weak do not exist as things to be used by the strong. Might does not make right. Slavery allows this. Institutional discrimination against other minorities — against Japanese-Americans in the Second World War and Hispanics even now, for example — allows this. All forms of injustice allow this, even when those who suffer are members of the majority. One has only to mention the centuries-long subjugation of women and the contemporary situation of the black population in South Africa.

The patent injustice of these arrangements needs no argument. Or so one must hope.

The situation of nonhuman animals in science (so-called "lab animals") is morally analogous to the king and his taster. We humans have the exalted status of royalty. Laboratory animals have the lowly status of our tasters. The difference is, they are called upon to do a great deal more than taste our food for us.

Perhaps as many as three animals die in laboratories every second. Just in the United States. Possibly twice that number worldwide. The reasons for this alarming rate of fatality vary. Sometimes these animals die in burn or brain trauma research. Sometimes they die as a result of tests on household products, such as oven cleaners or paint strippers. Sometimes they meet their death in high school or biology laboratories in the life sciences. The reasons for their death, in short, are as extensive as the ingenuity of the human mind. To the question, "Where will it all end?" the answer must be, "When the human mind runs out of new ways of using the powerless in the name of human interests." That doesn't seem like any time soon.

Genetic engineering is a case in point. We hear about its "advances" every day. Most people are unaware or indifferent to the nonhuman animals whose death and suffering often make this kind of "progress" possible. Most people see only the benefits. Few recognize the costs. After all, lab animals are our tasters, we humans their kings.

The essay that follows challenges this human arrogance. It focuses attention on the all but invisible role nonhuman animals are being forced to play in the burgeoning field of genetic engineering. But it also takes a broader view and examines the use of pigs in research on alcoholism, for example.

The position developed and defended in this essay applies the general principles that define the philosophy of animal rights to the issue of using nonhuman animals in science.

That philosophy is *categorically abolitionist* when it comes to this use of these animals.

That philosophy seeks to *keep these animals out of laboratories, totally,* not merely help insure their comfort while they're there. It is *empty,* not larger, cages that we demand.

That philosophy declares that any gains we receive from using these animals in science are *ill-gotten, not well-gotten.*

That philosophy insists that we humans have no greater moral right to use powerless animals as our tasters than kings had to use powerless human beings as theirs.

Enlightened people no longer grant such a privilege to royalty. The day will come when we deny the analogous privilege to the members of the scientific community.

_____

The last thing animals need are new reasons for exploiting them. They already have been drowned enough, shocked enough; burned, starved, bled enough; been socially deprived, blinded, rendered deaf and denied sleep enough; had their brains scrambled, their limbs severed, their internal organs crushed enough; suffered induced heart attacks, induced peptic ulcers, induced paralysis, induced epileptic seizures enough; been forcibly made to smoke cigarettes, drink alcohol, ingest heroine and cocaine enough; been used in enough high school science fairs, in enough college laboratories, in enough sessions of "practice" surgery; been living targets in enough tests of military weapons, irradiated in enough nuclear explosions, suffered enough in research in germ and chemical warfare;

been made to swallow enough brake fluid and carburetor cleaner, had their eyes blinded by enough paint stripper and face cleaners, had their bare skin exposed to enough caustic industrial and commercial chemicals and solvents. Animals, in short, as this all too brief inventory may at least suggest — animals have been systematically and relentlessly exploited in enough ways and in enough numbers that one would hope (for the sake of the animals) that we humans would have by now exhausted our enthusiasm if not our curiosity. But such is the ingenuity of the human mind that just when a moral optimist like myself would dare to hope that we might outgrow the sins of our fathers, what do we find but the spirit of inquiry reasserting itself.

There is a new incentive for animal exploitation being added to the already crowded agenda. Genetic engineering (so-called) has found an uncomprehending, powerless, and apparently limitless supply of "subjects" on which to devise and perfect its young ideas. It's all part of the "biotechnological revolution", a technological approach to agriculture, for example, described by the United States Department of Agriculture (USDA) in the following way:

> Biotechnology is broadly defined to include any technique that uses living organisms (or parts of organisms) to make or modify products, to improve plants or animals, or to develop microorganisms for specific use. New biotechnology techniques make it possible to move genes from one organism to another — a potential for mankind to alter genetic traits.

It all sounds rather exciting, certainly challenging. It also sounds just a bit scary. You put the results of such research, assuming it bears fruit, in the wrong hands, then quicker than you can say "Adolph Hitler" and you'll have the very serious threat, the very serious possibility of those slumbering yearnings about a "master race" reasserting themselves. It's the same kind of serious threat, the same kind of serious possibility we wince at when we think of today's nuclear weapons getting in the hands of terrorists with itchy trigger fingers and intimations of immortality. The social responsibility of scientists extends not only to those humans now alive but also to those yet to come —assuming we are not the last. It is a sobering thought, one that might have the power to delay, though probably not the strength to deny, the blossoming forth of the most fundamentally invasive form of science we have ever known.

My interest in gauging the threats posed by biotechnology includes but goes beyond the worries over what might become of us—us humans—if or as this revolution succeeds. As the USDA description points out, the techniques of biotechnology can be used to "improve...animals," where by 'animals' the authors evidently mean to exclude members of the species *Homo sapiens*. What does the word 'improve' mean here? Perhaps the best way to proceed is by way of example. So allow me to quote excerpts from a January 12, 1986 UPI story set in Athens, Ohio. The headline (as this appeared in *The Houston Post*) reads: "Genetic specialist predicts way to aid farmers, industry." "It's not nice to fool Mother Nature," the story begins, "but Tom Wagner is doing it every day. The Ohio University zoology professor", the story continues,

> is using "designer" genes to make pigs grow three times faster than normal, and he has planned a way to bottle genetic material for sale to farmers, who will then inject their own animals to enhance their good qualities...
>
> Through animal biotechnology, Wagner hopes to provide farmers with dream animals, all without having to feed them anything special.
>
> If you're a hog farmer and you get some pigs treated with fast-growth regulators, you will double the number of hogs you can take to market in a

year, sharply cut feed costs and make more economical use of your barns. Thus you can pay off debt faster on buildings and equipment.

For the consumer, the quick growth means pork with less fat and cholesterol...

The economic implications of this "genetic delivery" system are not lost on Ohio's state government, which has designated Wagner's project as one of six Advanced Technology Application Centers in Ohio and is pumping more than $3 million, matched by $4 million in federal funds, into the research.

I think this tells us rather well what it means to talk about "improving animals" in the present context. If hogs do not grow fast enough, could be raised more cheaply, or could produce a meat with less fat and cholesterol, then let us seek to discover the means to "improve" on lazy porcine metabolism. Or if hens do not lay enough eggs, or do not lay them fast enough, then let us find the genetic keys to unlock their ovarian sluggishness. And if dairy cattle do not produce enough milk, well, then let us find the way to overcome the udder limitations of bovine nature.

And if someone were to ask a researcher like Tom Wagner whether what he is doing is in the interests of the hogs, or the hens, or the dairy cattle, I think we understand that the question answers itself. Considerations about what's in the interests of these animals just aren't part of what it means to "improve" them. "What's-in-it-for-*these*-animals?" is no more a question that gets asked in this context than is true when rabbits are blinded with paint thinner, guinea pigs have their internal organs burst in the wake of being force-fed the latest version (the "new, improved" variety) of silver polish or hair spray, or Goobers (the chimp's name whose heart was transplanted into Baby Fae) becomes an all but anonymous part of medical history.

But who are we, we humans, to suppose that we are entitled to bypass this question about What's-in-this-for-these-animals? Who are we to claim the right to exploit animals in the ways we do, either the old ways of toxicity testing and learned helplessness experiments, for example, or the new ways of primate colonies for organ transplants and the genetic "improvement" of farm animals? No one (surely) will suggest that we have the right to exploit animals as we will merely because we have the power to do so. Might does not make right within the human moral community. Why should things be any different when we consider the moral community that includes the animals I've mentioned?

Perhaps some will be tempted to deny that there is such a moral community. After all, we belong to one species, these other animals belong to different ones. Morality, on the current view, holds only between the members of our species, not beyond it.

I don't think this view has anything more than prejudice on its side. The 17th century French philosopher René Descartes tried to dress this prejudice up in fancy rational clothes. He put animals outside the moral community on the grounds that only humans are aware of anything. Put a child's fingers in the fire and it hurts. Set fire to a cat and the cat feels nothing. Since the moral community for the Cartesian consists only of those who feel and are otherwise aware of things, we humans are in, nonhuman animals are out.

I must assume that no otherwise sensible person would today openly advocate the Cartesian view. Voltaire speaks well for all us ordinary folks when he asks the Cartesian whether "nature has arranged all the means of feeling (in the animals I've mentioned), so that (they) may not feel?" No, the physiology and behavior of these animals is just too much like our own to find it reasonable to maintain that we hear and smell and see, but they do not, or that we experience hunger, cold and fear, that we know the comfort of pleasure and the bite of pain, while they experience nothing. If all who feel and are aware are members of the moral community, then Tom Wagner's hogs and the other animals I've mentioned are in, not out.

There are familiar religious responses that attempt to exclude animals from the moral community. One rests on the dominion God is said to have given us over his creation, animals included. If 'dominion' is taken to mean 'subjugation,' and if the moral community excludes those whose very nature it is to be subjugated, then animals and the rest of God's creation are excluded from membership. But this surely has got the message all wrong. Creation was good before we humans came on the scene, according to the Genesis account, and the role God gave to us, the role of his vice-regent on earth, surely means that we are called upon to take care of his good creation in the name of his purposes, not in unrestrained pursuit of ours. The Anglican cleric Andrew Linzey expresses this point admirably when he states that "it is now commonly held... that although dominion involves the exercise of power, it is an exercise that must be subordinate to the moral purposes of God." "On a theistic understanding of creation, such as the Christian entertains," no less important members of the Anglican Church have written,

> it is a mistake to suppose that all animal life exists only to serve human kind; or that the world was made exclusively for man's benefit. Man's estimate of his own welfare should not be the only guideline in determining his relationship with other species. In terms of this theistic understanding man is custodian of the universe he inhabits with no absolute right over it.

Here, if not before, we will be told that animals lack immortal souls and that only those who have them belong to the moral community. Well, all this is controversial at best—controversial, first, because it is not certain that we humans have the requisite sort of soul and controversial, secondly, because it's uncertain that animals do not. For not only do we find attributions of souls to animals in many of the religions of the world — in Hinduism and Buddhism, for example — we also find an increasing number of Christian and other Western thinkers well disposed to the view that we humans are not unique in having the wherewithal to join the celestial chorus. In some elusive, possibly mystical sense, all of creation, including every animal other than the human variety, awaits the day of ultimate redemption — on this view.

But suppose the case is otherwise and that we humans are the only terrestrial species with immortal souls. What bearing could this possibly have on whether animals are members of the moral community here on earth? If Descartes was correct and animals felt nothing, then perhaps their cries and groans could be regarded as the morally indifferent sputterings of machines run afoul. But of course Descartes is not correct. The pains of animals are no less real than their eyes and ears. True, if they lack a soul, and if they therefore have no possibility of life after their terrestrial death, then there is nothing that can happen to them in a future state that would possibly compensate them for their earthly travails, including the misery they experience in human hands, not excluding the hands of the Tom Wagners of the world. But if that were true (as the influential Christian theologian C.S. Lewis saw), our duty to make their life good here on earth would not be lessened. On the contrary, this duty would be increased. I don't myself see how morally serious Christians (and the same applies to morally serious Jews) can avoid the conclusion that we need to get the hogs and other farm animals of the world out from under the tyranny of science. When the very idea of "improving animals" doesn't even include any mention of how the animals themselves will benefit, we can safely assume that, viewed from any credible theistic vantage-point, something has gone wrong.

Some there are who would accept the preceding and yet still put animals beyond the moral pale. The grounds they would invoke are biological in nature, broadly conceived. We are, according to this view, the apex of the biological world, the species towards which all of evolution has been inexorably moving. And just as we find that there is nothing wrong with the other species below us utilizing those species still lower than themselves, so we, the top-dog in the community of life, so to speak, are at liberty to utilize all those species below us in order to advance our own interests. If, then, the application of gene-splicing technology promises to further these interests, we are guilty of no wrong in using it.

This position, pervasive as it is in our secularized scientific community, commits just about all the textbook fallacies in moral theory. Suppose it is true that all the other species utilize species "below" them (whatever precisely that means). Then that is a fact. But from this fact (assuming it is one) it does not follow that we humans *ought* to utilize the species below us, or that we do nothing *wrong* if we do so. Neither values nor moral principles follow logically from facts. What *is* true *of* the world is not the same as, and does not entail, what *ought to be* true *in* it. Even if it were true (which of course it is not) that all human beings eat other animals, it would in no way follow that they ought to, or that they do nothing wrong in doing so. Questions of ethics are not questions of fact—at least not facts of the sort we can discover in, say, biology. Put another way, ethics is not one of the natural sciences. We need to ask moral questions about the scientific aspirations of the Tom Wagners of the world, not assume that their science itself provides us with the answers.

Still, biology is not irrelevant to working our way

toward some sensible ethical position concerning our
sometimes terminal scientific interactions with nonhuman
animals. Advocates of animal rights like myself sometimes argue that excluding animals from equal moral
consideration, denying then full membership in the
moral community, is in some ways analogous to such
prejudices as sexism and anti-Semitism. When people
hear this for the first time, they sometimes are shocked.
Some are even offended. But consider how Shakespeare
has Shylock, a Jew, address those Christians of his day
who were in the habit of discriminating against him.
"What's his reason?" Shylock asks of the Christian, and
then goes on to answer in these words:

> I am a Jew! Hath not a Jew eyes? Hath not a Jew
> hands, organs, dimensions, senses, affections, pas-
> sions? Fed with the same food, hurt with the same
> weapons, subject to the same diseases, healed by the
> same means, warmed and cooled by the same winter
> and summer as a Christian is? If you prick us, do we
> not bleed?...If you poison us, do we not die?...

James Gaffney, a Catholic ethicist at the University of
Loyola in New Orleans, offers the following telling insights
into Shakespeare's understanding of moral prejudice:

> ...in this savagely righteous denunciation of chron-
> ic injustice perpetrated by Christians upon Jews,
> what Shylock insists upon is not the Jew's human-
> ity but his animality, not his rationality but his
> organicity and sentiency, and not his capacity to
> be offended but his susceptibility to bodily hurt.
> He is thus able to make his moral point with great
> effectiveness without even risking his adversaries'
> contemptuous dismissal of any claim to human
> dignity. He strategically chooses the low ground
> because on that low ground even the most virulent
> anti-Semitism cannot obscure the justice of his
> complaint.

Gaffney, who is well aware of the astonishing dimensions of neglect of animals in Catholic theology — "how far Catholic moral theologians have been from (recognizing the moral claims of animals)," he writes, "may be drearily indicated by the fact that in most of their books, if there should occur any index reference to animals, it would probably lead the reader only to a portion of the treatise on lust dealing with the sin of bestiality!" — Gaffney goes on to add that "what for Shylock was the shrewdly chosen low ground must, I suppose, be considered the high ground for animals. But I do not see why that should make the same sort of argument morally unpersuasive when used in their behalf."

With that finding of Gaffney's I heartily concur, and the refusal to acknowledge the legitimate place of animals within the moral community or to deny them equal moral consideration because they belong to species other than our own would be no less a form of moral prejudice, and a moral prejudice of the same sort as a Christian's attempt to exclude Shylock because he was a Jew. We mean, then, those of us who champion the cause of animal rights, no insult to Jews or any other historically oppressed members of the human family when we liken the prejudice against nonhuman animals to the prejudices these humans have had to bear. Jews and blacks and other minorities — my own Irish forebears included — are not the less in our eyes because we see an analogy with the oppression of animals in their own oppression. Nor are animals the more in our eyes. Each is what each is. Nothing more. But nothing less. Each is one who has eyes, organs, affections, passions, one who knows warmth and cold, one who bleeds when pricked and dies when poisoned. Recognition of our shared animality marks the beginning of the new consciousness that underlies the struggle for animal rights.

But this marks the beginning only. Our shared animality is a fact. But facts are not values. The whole challenge of adequate theory construction in ethics remains. And on that topic the pressures of time oblige me to say little and to attempt to prove even less. Permit me to work my way towards my less ambitious conclusions by the following route.

Once we have accepted our shared animality with the hogs in Tom Wagner's care, for example, we need to ask whether we would accept the same kind of exploitation we find in his barn to continue if human beings were the subjects of his research. Would we, that is, tolerate the notion that Tom Wagner's brand of science really is "improving" human beings if he is able to get them to grow three times faster, produce cuts of meat that are lower in fat and cholesterol, and the rest of it. I must profoundly hope that none today would rise to vote in favor of this modest proposal. Human beings, even the weakest among us, do not exist for the purpose of someone else's gustatory delight or as tokens in some economic game called commercial human agriculture. Other humans, in other times and places, may have made a practice of eating their fellow *Homo sapiens,* but that fact was sufficient reason to confirm the identity of the chefs as savages or barbarians. We civilized folk have risen above all that. We wouldn't dream of doing the horrible things to humans we allow to be done to animals, whether on the farm or in the laboratory.

Well and good. As far as it goes. But does it go far enough? What could possibly be the defense of our savage exploitation of the animals in our care? I have explained why it cannot be any more reasonable to suppose that a difference in species could justify this than it would be to suppose that Christians were justified in exploiting Jews. Notions about who or what has a soul are no more effective as defenses, and our supposed God-given right to dominate the world should lead us, not to live off the backs of animals, as we in this culture do, but to try to stop those who do so. Our supposed position at the apex of the biological world is, at best, a fact, and facts never yield the answers to questions of value. What we do know is this: We allow to be done to nonhuman animals what we would not tolerate in the case of human animals. Yet both have eyes, and appetites, and passions, and pains, and pleasures, and are hurt, bleed, and die. I cannot see that we are anything but morally prejudiced and woefully inconsistent in our beliefs, attitudes and actions here. Heaven forbid that we should do to humans what now is being done to other animals. But heaven help us to stop doing these things to these animals.

For animals no more exist for us, to be used by us to promote our ends, however important these ends might be, than Jews exist for Christians, blacks for whites, or women for men. Animals are not our tasters. We are not their kings. It is time — long past time — that we recognize this elementary yet profound truth and bring consistency to our moral life. Even when it comes to how we treat pigs. For pigs are destined soon to become the experimental animal of choice in the era of biotechnology. "A new, improved (we know what *that* word means) miniature pig soon may be rooting its way into research labs," writes N. Scott Vance in the January 2, 1986 issue of *The Chicago Tribune*. "Charles River Laboratories of Massachusetts, the world's largest seller of lab animals," the story continues,

> early this year will unveil its trademarked Micropig — an 8-pound oinker that's billed as the perfect replacement for the hound. It's virtually hairless and friendly and doesn't provoke emotional protests.

Emotional protests from the American public, that is. At least that's the view of Michael Swindle of the Medical

University of South Carolina, a consultant to Charles River. Animal protection groups, according to Swindle, "have used the dog as America's sacred cow... They appeal for donations on the basis of our using dogs. But there will be little publicity or concern about using an animal in research...which everybody eats... We don't eat dogs. It's purely a perception thing." That much said, prospective clients might think a moment or two before trusting their dog to Dr. Swindle's care. But perhaps he is right about America's ethical sense: Dogs are special to us. Pigs are not. The proof, one might say, is in the eating. And the non-eating.

Or consider this story by Kathryn Eaker Perkins, writing in the December 19, 1985 edition of the *Sacramento Bee.*

> Charlotte, blonde and cute, is downright pig-gish: at 9 a.m. she downs her first cocktail of the day and snorts for more. She slurps the second and clamors for a third.
>
> She doesn't know when to stop and isn't alone. Hortense and Gertrude and Wilbur are just as unrestrained. Only Oscar obviously doesn't like the taste of alcohol. He stands quietly nursing his drink for an hour.

In case the plot isn't already obvious, the headline ("Pickled porkers on scholarly binge") and Ms. Perkins's next remarks remove all the mystery. What we have here is — science.

> The scene is not a neighborhood bar, but a laboratory at the University of California, Davis, where pigs are getting drunk.
>
> In fact, researchers from the medical school are leading these creatures down the path to alcoholism.
>
> It's all part of a scientific experiment to determine if alcoholics — who die by the tens of

thousands each year from malnutritional-related diseases — are able to absorb and metabolize nutrients from their food.

Within a week of the test's start, researchers expect the pigs to be consuming "the equivalent of 15 beers a day." The research is in its ninth year; rats and primates were used as test subjects prior to the arrival of Charlotte and the others. The protocol calls for a total of 45 pigs. Ms. Perkins relates that she asked Tony Buffington, a veterinarian working on this project, which is jointly funded by the National Institutes of Health and Bristol-Myers for $2-million, whether he "feels bad about turning these fastidious animals into alcoholics lolling in their waste and suffering hangovers." "You have to pretty carefully weigh what you do to animals in the interest of helping humans," he is reported to have replied.

Buffington may understand a good deal of science but one has to wonder about his abilities as a moral philosopher. Like other animal researchers, he seems to assume that animals such as pigs are just another sort of natural or genetically designed resource, born to be used in the name of the interest of a particular species — our species. But where there is no rational defense of a practice, there can be no reason to accept it as right. And there is no rational defense of our systematic, routinized, mechanized, and institutionalized exploitation of animals, pigs included.

Does this mean that animal rights activists take delight in the suffering of human beings? In the particular case of the alcoholics in our midst, are animal rights activists only too happy to let them make it through their rocky life on their own, without any medical assistance? Here again the questions answer themselves. Those who care about the rights of animals cannot fail to care about the health of human beings. We should do what we morally can do to help the sick — by giving greater funding to alcohol abuse centers and psychological support facilities, for example, and increased funding for preventive programs; help that goes directly to the people who need it most and need it most immediately, not to speculative and all but hopeless research on alcoholic animals. A Christian who refused to support experiments on Jews would not prove how little he loved his fellow Christians. He would only show how much he respected the rights of Jews. Logically and morally, the case is no different with the animals I've mentioned. We who would have our science respect the rights of animals do not love our fellow humans the less. It is justice we respect the more, a justice that transcends the boundaries of our own species. By all means, then, let us reap the gains our science can yield — provided only that they are well- not ill-gotten.

When the dust settles and the opposing sides have had their say, Dr. Swindle's remark, the one about, "It's purely a perception thing," still lingers. There is an element of wisdom here. For if we could see the animals in our laboratories differently, if we could reach a point of expanded consciousness where we sensed their beauty and dignity, their individual integrity and their moral kinship with us, then we would, perhaps, put an end to our own species' variation on the theme of bestiality. Such depth of perception was reached by Leonardo da Vinci, for example. Recall his monumental words: "The time will come when men such as I will look upon the murder of animals as we now look upon the murder of men." St. Francis, too, acquired that vision. His words and deeds are legendary, and rightfully so. Of course you and I are not required to raise ourselves to his ecstatic heights or to talk with our animal brethren before we can learn to recognize the massive scale of our exploitation of them for the great wrong that it is:

> *3 animals killed every second in laboratories in the United States, probably twice that number worldwide.

*5 *billion* animals killed annually for food, just in America.

*15 million unclaimed and unwanted companion animals "put to sleep" annually in our pounds and shelters in the United States — and some 200,000 of these animals, the even less lucky ones, are sold to researchers to meet their death in one lab or another, in one experiment or another.

*$7 billion of federal support of animal-related research poured annually into the powerful wheels of the medical-industrial complex, a figure approaching almost $2 million dollars every hour of every day — just in the United States.

Historically considered, there is perhaps only one other massive human evil to compare with it, one that I, as a gentile, would not allude to on my own initiative. But Isaac Bashevis Singer, the Pulitzer Prize winning novelist, himself a Jew, has. There is, he says, another Holocaust occurring, right before our eyes, only in this one it is nonhuman, not human animals, who are the victims.

When viewed against the staggering numbers involved, with figures in the billions, it is perhaps difficult to see the evil being done to Charlotte and Hortense and the other 40-odd pigs being encouraged to consume the equivalent of fifteen beers a day. Perhaps our perception gets numbed by the sheer volume of the abuse. And so we look for help, for guidance so that we might better see and appreciate the desperate plight of Charlotte and the other "pickled porkers." And when we look, if we do, we find the help, the guidance in the person of St. Francis. For one of the animals into whose depths he saw and whose beauty he understood was a pig — a sow. I shall leave you with a reminder of his sense of this oft-misunderstood and much maligned creature, the one whose micro-sized off-spring will be filling up the cages of our laboratories in the near future — in the name of "progress." St. Francis's loving perception of this animal is a vision to be compared with Tom Wagner's, Tony Buffington's, Michael Swindle's, and the rest of the people who comprise the medical-industrial complex. None are so blind as those who will not see.

5

The Other Victim

Occasionally a medical story unfolds that attracts massive media attention. Barney Clark's heroic struggle to survive the first mechanical heart transplant is a case in point. So, too, is the no less celebrated story of Baby Fae, the infant girl who received the heart of a baboon named Goobers. Both Barney Clark and Baby Fae have earned permanent places in the history of medicine. Our children, and our children's children, will be taught about them.

Of the two cases, the one involving Baby Fae is the most directly relevant to the Animal Rights Movement. Everyone involved in the struggle for animal rights has been challenged by hostile critics who say that we favor nonhuman animals above human beings. We are charged with being misanthropic (literally, people who hate humanity). These critics ask, "What would you do if you had to choose between saving the life of a child and that of a dog, a cat, a rat, or a baboon?" The answer they want, and the one they like to use in their fund-raising campaigns, is that we'd save the animal.

Small wonder, then, that the case of Baby Fae seemed as if it was custom made for the enemies of animal rights. Who but a misanthrope could protest saving Baby Fae instead of some anonymous baboon? Any academic like myself, who chose to speak out for the rights of the baboon in this case, risked public ridicule and loss of professional standing. Only an "animal crazy" could favor the baboon above the baby.

Despite these risks, I did speak out in favor of the rights of Goobers, and my reasons for doing so are set out in the brief essay that follows. I don't think it reads like the crazed rantings of a misanthrope. Only the most calloused could have failed to have felt pity for Baby Fae and empathy for her caring parents. I cared very much, and so did every other person I know who is involved in the struggle for animal rights. It was not *we* who failed to care enough about Baby Fae. *We* wanted her interests well served. Tragically, they were not. Also tragically, neither were the interests of the other victim, Goobers.

If any good arose from this double tragedy, perhaps it is simply this: That those of us who struggle for animal rights were able to denounce the ethics of killing the baboon in the vain attempt to save an innocent little girl, without either being or appearing misanthropic. We wanted Baby Fae to live, which was part of our reason for not wanting to have the baboon killed. The enemies of animal rights were silenced by the logic of our informed opposition. To be for the rights of animals never is to be opposed to the rights of human beings.

"The Other Victim" originally appeared in *The Hastings Center Report* of February 1985 and is reprinted here with the kind permission of the editor.

Like most people, my heart broke when Baby Fae died. It was no good my telling myself that thousands of babies die every day. Baby Fae was special. A member of our extended family, she was a child of the nation. When she died, we all grieved.

Others on this occasion will be drawn to debate the ethics of her treatment. I shall not here defend, only voice, my conviction that she was not treated fairly, that her interests were not uppermost in the aspirations of her principal caregivers. On this occasion I am pulled in another direction. For, unlike some people, my heart broke twice during Baby Fae's public struggle. There were two victims in my view, not just one; though, like the proverbial black cat in the dark room, the other victim was easy to overlook.

In grieving Baby Fae's death, we were on familiar ground. She was *somebody,* a distinct individual with an unknown but partly imaginable future. If we allowed ourselves, we could share her first taste of ice cream, feel the butterflies in her stomach before the third grade play, endure her braces. When we consider the other victim, the baboon, the landscape changes. That lifeless corpse, the still beating heart wrenched from the uncomprehending body: for some people that death marks the end, not of somebody, but of some *thing.* A member of some species. A model. A tool. A token of a type. After all, there were no braces, there was no junior prom, in that brute creature's future.

Lack of empathy for the baboon is not easily improved upon. Even to note its absence or, more boldly, to suggest the appropriateness of our grieving over "its" death will meet with stiff incredulity in some quarters. When the choice is between a baby and a baboon, can there be any question? Really?

However natural it may seem to answer "no", I think we must answer "yes." It is true that Goobers (though seldom used, this was the baboon's name) had a quite different potential, a quite different future form of life than Baby Fae. But no one, surely, will seriously question whether the duration and quality of his life mattered to that animal. Surely no one will seriously suggest that it was a matter of indifference to Goobers whether he kept his heart or had it transferred to another. Are we not yet ready to see that creatures such as baboons not only are alive, they have a life to live?

Perhaps the weary charges of "anthropomorphism" will fill the air. Baboons feel pain, it may be allowed. But their sentience exhausts their psychology. A twinge of discomfort here, maybe a warm stroke of pleasure there; that about does it.

This sparse view of baboon psychology will not stand up under the weight of our best thinking, neither philosophical nor scientific. Baboons not only feel pain, they *prefer* to avoid it, *remember* what it is like, *intentionally* seek to avoid it, *fear* its source. To describe and explain baboon behavior in such mentalistic terms is intelligible, confirmable, and defensible. As Darwin saw, and as we should see, the psychology of such creatures differs from ours in degree, not in kind. Like us, Goobers was *somebody,* a distinct individual. He was the experiencing subject of a life, a life whose quality and duration mattered to him, independently of his utility to us.

Suppose this is true. Where does it take us morally? Everything depends on how firm the moral status of experiencing subjects-of-a-life is believed to be. You are such a subject, and so am I. Morally, I do not believe that you exist *for me,* as my resource, to be used by me to forward my own or, for that matter, someone else's interests. And, of course, I do not believe that I exist as your resource either. Just as I would violate your right to be treated with respect if I forced my will on you in the name of promoting my own or anyone else's welfare, so you would do the same to me if you treated me similarly. This sort of strict equality between us, viewed as experiencing subjects-of-a-life, is, I believe, the fundamental precept in terms of which the morality of all our interactions ultimately must be gauged.

I would appeal to this precept to defend my opposition to using a healthy Baby Fae's heart to save the life of a sick Goobers. She did not exist as his resource. But I would insist upon equal treatment for Goobers. He did not exist as her resource either. Those people who seized his heart, even if they were motivated by their concern for Baby Fae, grieviously violated Goobers' right to be treated with respect. That he could do nothing to protest, and that many of us failed to recognize the transplant for the injustice that it was, do not diminish the wrong, a wrong settled before Baby Fae's sad death. Fundamental moral wrongs are not alterable by future results. Or past intentions.

What, then, can we do when, as is certain, we face other Baby Faes whose life hangs by a thread? Morally and medically, we must do everything we may, balancing, as best we can, the vital interests present in health care contexts such as these against those we find in others. With limited resources, we cannot, alas, do everything it would be good to do. What we must not do, either now or in the future, is violate the rights of some in order to benefit others. Our gains must be well- not ill-gotten. One measure of our medical progress will be the number of Baby Faes we are able to keep alive. But our resolve not to kill future Goobers will be one measure of our moral growth.

6

Against Sealing

The struggle for animal rights is not for the faint of heart. It takes dedication, patience, and endurance to work for their rights, not just a few hours here and there but most of one's waking life, day in and day out. All of us involved in this struggle must daily reaffirm our commitment and squarely face that other struggle we all have to deal with — the struggle with ourselves, especially the temptation to give up, to quit. One has to wonder, sometimes, whether all the time and effort are worth it, whether anything we do ever makes any real difference.

Well, it *is* worth it, of course, and our collective efforts *do* make a difference, even if not as much as we want. In case we need something to demonstrate this fact, we only need to consider the impact we have had on the Canadian sealing industry. What was once a $12 million business (that's the 1982 figure) is now all but bankrupt — "floating belly up in the water," as we might say. Why? Not because the sealers lost interest in their trade. And not because the Canadian government has decided to remove its support. No, this industry is all but finished because of the hard work of people in our Movement.

Consciousness has been raised about the grotesque annual slaughter of baby seals off the coast of Newfoundland, and with that increase in consciousness has come an outpouring of compassion, from all corners of the world. The result? The former lucrative market in "white coats" is all but dried up. And where there is no demand, there will be no supply, either.

My own involvement in this process included prepared testimony I presented before the Royal Commission on Seals and the Sealing Industry. I was one of a number of Americans who had the privilege to make a submission to this body in March of 1985, in Washington, D.C. Friends from England and Canada had written and phoned me to say that the Commission was "stacked" in favor of the sealing industry, a "puppet" of that industry, a "public relations ploy." There was, I was told, absolutely no chance that my views would be taken seriously.

Well, my views were taken seriously. Members of the Royal Commission first listened respectfully to my prepared statement, then proceeded to question me for the better part of an hour. The questions were fair, to the point, and asked in a constructive spirit. I like to think that the members came ready to learn about and to appreciate all sides to the controversy.

As of this writing the Royal Commission has yet to release its final report. The most recent news suggests that the report will call for government compensation to cover the losses suffered by the sealers (a policy I introduced and supported in my presentation) along with further government support of the commercial harvesting of seals after they pass the white coat stage (a policy I implicitly opposed). Whatever the final recommendations of the Commission, chances are that we haven't heard the last of the sealing industry. There is tremendous pressure not to be defeated by our Movement, pressure that arises from sources outside, not just inside, the sealing industry itself. We have won some big battles. Now we must be certain we don't lose the war. Eternal vigilance is required no less from us, to protect the rights of nonhuman animals, than it is required of everyone, if we are to protect the basic rights of human beings.

Ethical progress is never easy. We would be better at it, if it were. Such progress requires change, both change in what we do and in what we cease to do. When we call for change in others, without having to make any changes ourselves, the progress may seem simple. But it never is, and we must never forget this. When, therefore, in what follows, I add my voice to those who call for an end to commercial sealing, for ethical reasons, I hope I will not be misperceived as one who lacks sympathy for commercial sealers, or as one who would shower them with malice and contempt. I understand, as well as my imagination enables me, that but for some contingencies of birth and location, time and custom, I would be one of them. Then *I* would be the one called upon to change. And I do not have much difficulty in imagining how difficult that change would be.

Underlying the call for an end to commercial sealing is a growing change in the perception of what seals are. So long as there was no serious challenge to viewing these animals as a renewable natural resource, whose place in the scheme of things was to serve human interests, there could be no serious ethical challenge to commercial sealing. The serious ethical challenge now being raised is symptomatic of a fundamental change in our perception of these animals.

This change has come about in response to a range of questions, including the following: Are seals aware of anything? Are they capable of experiencing pain or enjoying themselves? Do they have biological and social needs which they take pleasure in satisfying? Do individual animals have an identity over time, so that it makes sense to think of them as faring well or faring ill as their life goes on?

When these questions are asked, I believe they have rationally compelling answers: Seals are aware of a great deal; they are capable of experiencing pain and of enjoying themselves; they do take pleasure in satisfying their biological and social needs; and they do have an individual welfare of their own. In *these* respects — but not, of course, in *all* respects — these animals are like human beings.

Against this backdrop, the larger structure of the debate over the ethics of commercial sealing can be seen more clearly. Whereas some people see seals as stocks or herds, with quotas to be harvested or populations to be cropped, others (myself included) see them as *individuals,* each one of which has a life of its own to live — a life of importance to the individual whose life it is, quite independently of how useful that individual is to others.

And this new perception of these animals has given rise to a new understanding of the ethical ties that bind us to them. Seals no more exist for us, as our resources, given this new understanding, than I exist for you, as your resource. True, we humans can — and we have — treated seals as if they are ours, just as we humans can — and have — treated other human beings in analogous ways. But to treat other human beings as if the whole point of their existence is to be our resource, put here on earth to serve our ends or to fulfill our purposes, is the very paradigm of human exploitation. The might to do this does not make it right to do. The emerging ethical challenge to commercial sealing merely extends this line of reasoning to include the seals. To treat these animals as if the whole point of their existence is to be our resource, is a new paradigm of animal exploitation; and the might to do this does not make this right to do either.

Were I a commercial sealer, I believe my initial reaction to this reasoning would be to protest against my critics. Do they object to my role in the harvesting of seals over a dinner of veal parmigiana perhaps? Then they have a rather strange notion of ethics, one that requires change by me but no change by them. Let them get their own moral house in order first, before they spend their leisure time trying to rearrange mine.

Were I a commercial sealer, I hope I would not be satisfied with this response, however natural it might be. For the ethical heart of the matter is not how well my critics practice what they preach; what matters is the truth of what they say. If commercial sealing is wrong, then it ought to be stopped. And the truth of this claim —'It ought to be stopped' — does not change in the slightest if the people who make it support other practices that wrongfully exploit animals. If my critics are morally inconsistent and weak, it does not follow that I must be. That, I hope, is the insight I would come to have, if I happened to be a commercial sealer. I would want to act on the truth of the ethical claim, not worry over the ethics of those who make it.

What those who argue for an end to commercial sealing owe to commercial sealers is not our vindictiveness —as if our hands are morally clean, theirs alone morally dirty. What we owe them is our compassion. Our understanding. Our empathy for them, caught, as they are, between the end of one tradition and the beginning of another. And our help. The world grows weary of militance and meanness. Our moral task is to help the seals, not hurt the sealers. Surely this *can* be done, once we share the vision that it *ought* to be. For the means must be discovered after we have settled on the desirability of the end. Not before.

It would be more than a little presumptuous of me to tell you what these means are. To establish them requires knowledge I do not have. My contribution, offered in good faith, concerns the ethics of the end for which we should labor, one that includes the demise of commercial sealing in Canada — but without assaulting the humanity of Canadian sealers or the integrity of their nation and government.

7

The Abolition of Pound Seizure

No issue puzzles me more than that of pound seizure — by which I mean the sale or surrender of unwanted companion animals by pounds (or shelters) to dealers, who in turn sell them to be used for a variety of scientific purposes, including toxicity testing and instruction (especially in the so-called "dog lab"). What puzzles me so much is why the scientific establishment would risk so much to gain so little. For there are few, if any, uses of animals that can rival pound seizure in terms of the potential for calling forth the public's rage against science and its practitioners. Comparatively few people love hogs or chickens. Many, many more love cats and dogs. And these latter animals are the ones who are the victims of pound seizure. An informed, aroused public, or even just a good slice of those who have companion animals, surely could make scientists rue the day they ever got themselves identified with supporting this disgraceful practice.

And yet scientists by and large persist in their support. On the occasion when I presented the remarks reproduced below, there were ten of us who had a few minutes each to speak against pound seizure, and there were the others who spoke in favor. (The occasion was before a meeting of a subcommittee of the North Carolina

General Assembly back in 1985.) Those on the animals' side were the usual people — someone from a shelter, a "pet owner," an animal activist. Those on the opposing side also were the usual people — the Deans of the Schools of Medicine at East Carolina University, the University of North Carolina at Chapel Hill, and Bowman Gray School of Medicine, and — of course — high administrators of the School of Veterinary Medicine, North Carolina State University.

The power of the status quo won that day. Pound seizure is still perfectly legal in North Carolina, as it is in most states. But not for long. This *is* one issue we most certainly will win in our lifetime. And when we do, a great deal more than the use of pound animals will have changed. Because the research establishment has so adamantly aligned itself with those who favor pound seizure, repeal will be seen as a defeat for scientists and a victory for us. And that will give our cause an added boost we could not have gotten on our own. There are few blessings we can count as ours, and always there is the gnawing, awful truth of animal suffering and death. But at least we have the foolishness of the scientific establishment, when it comes to picking battles, to be thankful for.

The issue of pound seizure is sometimes misrepresented. It is not a matter of being for or against using any animals in science. It is the use of a particular, identifiable sub-class of animals — namely, unwanted or unclaimed pet animals in our state's pounds and shelters — it is whether these animals are to be used in science that is the issue. And people can be against using these animals without having to oppose using all animals, just as, for example, people can oppose some taxes without having to oppose all taxes.

Neither is the issue of pound seizure one that requires us to decide whether we are pro- or anti-science. People can oppose the use of pound animals in science without denying the contributions scientists make, just as, analogously, people can favor limiting the size of trucks on our highways without denying the benefits attributable to the trucking industry.

The issue of pound seizure, in other words, is only confusedly thought of as a pro- vs. anti-vivisection, or a pro- vs. anti-science debate. And though this should be obvious to everyone, past experience teaches that it needs to be noted at the outset. For proponents of allowing pound seizure sometimes argue for their position by misrepresenting their opponents'. They say their opponents must be anti-vivisectionists. Must be anti-scientific. But that is not true. To be against pound seizure is not the same as being against vivisection, let alone against science.

Pound seizure is a difficult moral issue. And, like any such issue, it cannot be understood in isolation. Fifteen million unwanted or unclaimed companion animals are killed each year in America's pounds and shelters. Approximately one every two seconds. Almost 2,000 every hour, 24 hours a day, day in and day out. Who can take pride in these numbers? No one in this room, I am certain. And no one in this state. For if these depressing numbers could speak, they would shout at us, accusing us — and rightly so — of a colossal moral failure, as a nation and as a state. We are just not very good at carrying out our end of the arrangement struck with our companion animals. True, as individuals we may love and care for those animals in our trust, may treat them, as indeed they are, as honorary members of our household. But collectively, when our human failures are computed alongside our individual successes, our record is one of tragic irresponsibility.

That is part of the larger setting in which the issue of pound seizure must be viewed — against the backdrop of our collective irresponsibility. The millions of animals in our shelters are there because of human decision and negligence. That point is both brutally simple and incontrovertible.

What ought we to do with these animals? Advocates of pound seizure recommend that we be allowed to use some for research purposes. This would be to make the best of a bad thing, they think. Since these animals are destined to die soon anyway, why not get something positive out of their death? It just makes sense, or so it is claimed.

But it does not make sense. More than anything else, allowing pound seizure undermines the historic moral mission of our pounds and shelters. That mission is simple: to serve as the last safe haven for animals who are the victims of human irresponsibility. And that mission is flagrantly undermined when, as pound seizure allows, animals pass through our shelters' doors and into our state's laboratories.

What citizen can — what citizen should — have confidence in the integrity of our shelters when this can happen? Why should we believe that we do best by unwanted, lost or abandoned animals when we turn them over to our pounds if they in turn can serve as a halfway house between us and our state's research laboratories? Pound seizure undermines this historic trust and, in so doing, undermines the historic mission of the shelters themselves.

Legally to allow pound seizure is publicly to confess that we no longer have the resolve to carry out this mission — that we will no longer do what is best for the pathetic products of human irresponsibility. To allow it, then, is to diminish ourselves... to make ourselves less worthy of respect... so that the issue of pound seizure — the fundamental issue — is not whether we are for or against animal rights. It is whether we are for or against what is best in ourselves.

Defenders of pound seizure will say that the price of research will go up if scientists are denied ready access to pound animals. Should we believe this? I don't think so. For there are studies, done by reputable folks, that show that use of pound animals actually costs more than use of so-called purpose-bred animals. But however this cost-benefit issue is decided, the issue of pound seizure is not just a matter of dollars and cents... and I say this even if it is demonstrated, beyond a reasonable doubt, that economy is on the side of making pound seizure illegal in North Carolina. At issue, as I have indicated — at least in my view and I hope in yours — is the historic moral charge to a valued institution... our animal shelters. And the symbolic and real value of this institution to North Carolinians, like the symbolic and real value of the other treasured institutions in our State, is not reducible to dollars and cents. Our shelters are part of our heritage. And we North Carolinians do not reduce the value of our heritage to money. At least I hope we do not.

Defenders of pound seizure will say that, not just money, the quality of scientific research and education depends on ready access to pound animals in North Carolina. Those who deny this either are uninformed or emotionally out of control, or so it is implied. Should we believe this?

Well, here is a simple, conclusive test, I think. Let us consider the states that prohibit pound seizure. And let us ask whether the educational and research institutions in these states are demonstrably inferior to those we find in North Carolina. Here are some of the states:

> Pennsylvania, Rhode Island, Connecticut, New Jersey, Hawaii, New York, and Massachusetts.

And here is a sampling of the schools of human medicine

we find in these locations:

> Tufts University, Rutgers University, Syracuse University, Albert Einstein School of Medicine, Yeshiva University, Mt. Sinai School of Medicine, University of Pittsburgh, Cornell University, Columbia University, the University of Pennsylvania, Yale University, Princeton University, and Harvard University.

And, in veterinary medicine and science:

> Cornell University, the University of Pennsylvania, Pennsylvania State University, Tufts University, and the University of Massachusetts at Amherst.

As for research centers in these states, the list numbers in the many hundreds, including:

> The Boston Biomedical Research Institute, The Boston University Hubert H. Humphrey Cancer Research Center, The Boston University Multipurpose Arthritis Center, The Columbia University Comprehensive Sickle Cell Center, The Harvard University Pediatric Pulmonary Laboratory, Helen Keller International, The Massachusetts Institute of Technology, Laboratory for Biomechanics and Human Rehabilitation, The New York University Cancer Center, Princeton University Department of Biochemical Sciences, Rutgers University Center of Alcoholic Studies, University of Pennsylvania Institute of Neurological Sciences, University of Pittsburgh Cystic Fibrosis Research Center, University of Rochester Center for Brain Research, Yale University Comprehensive Cancer Center, and the Diabetes, Cancer, Genetics, and Liver Research Centers at Yeshiva University.

Like other North Carolinians, I am proud of the many noteworthy accomplishments of our State's medical schools and research centers. But my pride is not blind.

And neither I hope is yours. There simply is no good reason to believe that scientific education and research in the states I mentioned are inferior to what we have in North Carolina because we allow, while they prohibit, pound seizure.

I have mentioned pride a number of times. To my mind, that is the heart of the matter: Pride in our State —pride in its institutions and laws — a pride born of our commitment to take our heritage seriously. We who live in North Carolina like to think of our State as progressive in the best sense — as a leader, economically, culturally, educationally, morally. We cannot be the first State in America to lead the way by prohibiting the sale of pound animals, just as America was not the first nation to do so. (Such sales are uniformly banned in, for example, England and Sweden.) The other states I've mentioned are a step ahead. But we can be the first state in our region to join them and so serve as a worthy symbol of progressiveness for our near neighbors. It would be a modest triumph of principle perhaps. But of such triumphs are a state's reputation made.

8

The Role of Culture in the Struggle for Animal Rights

Here's a menu of verbal abuse that's familiar to everyone involved in the struggle for animal rights.

"People who care about animals are too emotional."

"Animal lovers are mostly uneducated and uninformed."

"It's all right to be kind to animals, but people who say animals have rights are crazy!"

"Advocates of 'animal liberation' are sick."

These entrees could be expanded tenfold, but each new one would merely be a variation on the same theme. That theme is simple. It's that people who advocate animal rights just don't have their heads screwed on right. We are "sick," "weird," "crazy," "ignorant," "illogical," "emotional," or (I kid you not — this actually has been said) "part of the communist conspiracy"! As if the ruthless violation of the rights of animals was unique to capitalism.

This verbal war would be comic if it weren't for the tragedy in the background. Those of us who struggle for animal rights can take the abuse. We're used to it. But the animals are in a different situation. They shouldn't have to endure the pain and death human greed and curiosity demand. This isn't a laughing matter. It is, one might say

— and one *should* say this — a matter of life and death.

As I said in my introductory remarks to "The Case for Animal Rights" (see above), I am of the old school: I believe the best defense is a good offense. And *one* form a good offense can take is to post a series of reminders, a set of references and quotes that help the literate public recall the *identity* of various people who have been involved in the struggle for animal rights. The aim is simple: We want the public to know and appreciate *who said what,* when this is favorable to our Movement.

This way of taking the offensive is not an argument for the truth of the animal rights philosophy. That is given in the philosophical works that help define our Movement (in *The Case for Animal Rights,* for example). No, this way of taking the offensive (the posting of reminders) is different. It simply asks the literate public to make some informed decisions.

Was Leonardo da Vinci (he was a committed vegetarian, for moral reasons) "crazy"? Was Mark Twain (he was an abolitionist regarding the use of nonhuman animals in science, again for moral reasons) part of the "communist conspiracy"?

The logic of this way of taking the offensive isn't hard to figure out. Any remotely intelligent human being will answer these questions with a resounding "No!" And every halfway sensible person will therefore begin to realize that it can't be fair, can't be rational, must be "emotional" to categorize *all* animal rights advocates as "crazy," "weird," "agents of the communist conspiracy" — or worse. On the contrary, every semi-literate person will begin to get the idea that *it is the opponents of animal rights* who give more than episodic evidence of being "illogical," "uninformed," "emotional," and so on. And that, of course, is precisely why this way of taking the offensive *is* a very good defense. It shifts the burden of false accusations onto the accuser. It's the moral equivalent of judo.

The essay that follows is an example of this other way of taking the offensive. It isn't the last word. Maybe it isn't even the first. But it might do some good. Never underestimate the importance of having gifted, talented, and famous individuals associated with the struggle for animal rights. Some people respond to names more readily than they respond to ideas. It's important to realize the deep, powerful resources we have in this regard.

How important are these resources? Well, important enough for me, at least, to give this part of our Movement the major portion of my time. Twain and da Vinci are dead. Rachel Rosenthal and Matt Tasley are alive. And so are numerous other gifted artists and thinkers. A vital part of our Movement's future depends on how well we identify and support the gifted hands, voices, and minds who express positive concern for animals in their work —in their painting, theatre preformances, dance, poetry, legal and moral theory: in the broad sweep of *cultural endeavor.* That's what the Culture & Animals Foundation (CAF) is all about. That's CAF's agenda. We don't intend to fail.

Those of us involved in the struggle for animal rights *are* part of what is best in the world, not a throwback to what is worst. *We* know that. We have *always* known that. Our challenge now is to insure that the public does, too. One small way to meet this challenge is to be a "name dropper." That's the small step I take in this essay.

It's always good to be part of something good. And it's better by far to have a hand in success rather than failure. That's why those of us involved in the struggle for animal rights have at least two solid reasons for taking some satisfaction in what we are doing. For make no mistake about it: We *are* on the side of what is good. And we *are* succeeding.

The signs of success are everywhere. In the classroom, for example. Not long ago the very idea of animal rights would have been laughed out of our halls of learning — if anyone had even dared mention it. But times have changed. In philosophy, for example, where before there were none, now there are perhaps 100,000 students a year discussing animal rights. Animal rights is in philosophy classrooms because the idea is in philosophy textbooks. And it's in philosophy's textbooks because philosophers have taken the idea seriously enough to write about it.

This same kind of transformation, from no students to tens of thousands discussing animal rights, is beginning to take place in other academic subjects. In law, for example, and even in anthropology and introductory composition. The logic of this change is everywhere the same. Material about animal rights is showing up first in the professional literature, then in the textbooks, and ultimately in the classroom. Those simple facts make all the difference in the world. They are a tangible, powerful sign of the growing success of our movement. They give our cause legitimacy.

Changes in the halls of Congress are no less a tribute to our success. Not very long ago people in Washington ran for cover if someone talking about "animal rights" paid a visit. Whatever the visitor had to say, it *couldn't* make any sense. That was the dominant view. Doors were closed, sometimes not very quietly.

Today those doors increasingly are open. Animal rights is recognized as a *serious* political issue — the sort of issue that means votes when election time rolls around. And *more* each time people cast their ballots. Writing in the March 1, 1986 issue of *The Lancet,* David McKie observes that "for increasing numbers of young (English)

voters, animal rights belong not on the fringes of the
political debate, but right at the heart of it...The political
momentum...is growing year by year." The American
political process isn't any different. Animal rights has
come in from the cold to become a part of the hot moral
agenda of middle-America. That means power. Animal
rights activists are getting the political respect they
deserve.

Even the religious community, once thought to be
categorically opposed to animal rights, grows steadily
more responsive. Thoughtless exploitation of animals is
today seen for the great offense to God and God's creation
it has always been. Our deadly sins know no species
boundary. The same evil impulses that lead people to
victimize the least powerful of our human brothers and
sisters lead them to abuse the least of these — our cousins,
the animals. Cruelty to humans and cruelty to animals are
cut fromt eh same defective cloth, which is why the
religious community is beginning to recognize that we
won't make any serious advance on the momentous
problems of "man's inhumanity to man" if we fail to
address our unhumanity to animals.

All these changes — and more — *are* taking place, *are*
part of our emerging power, and *are* symptoms of our
growing success. And yet valuable though they are each
leaves important stones unturned. Despite these advances
the public's image of the Movement remains largely the
one the media serve up. And that image is one of nay-
saying, not yea-saying, of people who are against, not
people who are for, of largely uneducated kooks pitted
against the priestly caste of modern intellectual life —
physicians and research scientists, for example.

Why many people continue to view the Movement's
members in these ways is easy to explain. The media, both
print and video, thrive on plane crashes, calamity and
conflict, not peace and quiet. What whets the media's appe-

tite is confrontation, not rigorous thought. Just try getting on TV to present the *philosophy* of animal rights in an emotionally uncharged atmosphere, free of unsympathetic hosts or hostile panelists. No, the media like us when we're chanting and protesting, not when we're speaking softly and carrying the big stick of reason.

The false image of who we are and what we stand for is the biggest obstacle standing in the way of our making a quantum leap in terms of our power to effect social change. There's just no getting around that fact. But there are ways to get over it. We must learn to present the truth about ourselves and our vision. This will require that we ourselves become conversant with the deep, abiding cultural foundations on which we stand. We are not the last to proclaim the rights of animals. But neither are we the first. Great men and women from the past, people of real genius and accomplishment, have shared our values and expressed them in both word and deed. If we are to alter our present image in the media, if we are to educate the public about our true identity, then we must use every available opportunity to reveal our cultural heritage. For ours *is* the message of the finest minds, the most gifted hands.

In the case of hunting and other blood sports, for example, we need to have the Oscar Wildes of the world as our constant companions. Wilde's famous description of fox-hunting ("The unspeakable in full pursuit of the uneatable") captures well the condemnation of hunting and other blood sports shared by everyone in our Movement. This same spirit burns though the lines of Walter de la Mare's jolly little poem, "Hi", which tells the story of a "handsome hunting man" who kills an animal with a gun, and concludes with the (sarcastic) line, "Oh, what fun!"

True, there are occasional miscreants — the Hemingways of the world, who glorify in their conquest of animals what they are unable to conquer in themselves. On this matter, as on others, John Steinbeck's insight should prevail:

> We have never understood why men mount heads of animals...possibly it feels good to these men to be superior to animals, but does it not seem that if they were sure of it they would not have to prove it?
> *The Sea of Cortez*

The eighteenth century English poet William Cowper makes a similar point in his poem "The Task":

> Detested sport
> That owes its pleasure to another's pain;
> That feeds upon the sobs and dying shrieks
> Of harmless nature, dumb, but yet endued
> With eloquence, that agonies inspire,
> Of silent tears, and heart-distending sights!
>
> The heart is hard in nature, and unfit
> For human fellowship as being void
> Of sympathy, and therefore dead alike
> To love and friendship both, that is not
> pleased
> With sight of animals enjoying life,
> Nor feels their happiness augment his
> own...

In another of his poems, entitled "Tit for Tat", Walter de la Mare takes us down an imaginary road towards retributive justice — the day when the poem's protagonist, the "sportsman" Tom Noddy, gets his due. "An Ogre" from another planet hunts and kills Tom Noddy, places him on a hook where he glares "in an empty stare," and finally is cooked himself.

Perhaps some people who are not yet part of our Movement will say, "But hunting and other blood sports are easy targets. What about medical research — cases where we humans have benefited or are likely to do so in the future. Here surely there is only room for the opposition of ignorant fanatics — irresponsible misanthropes who can't count to ten without using their fingers."

Well, is that a fair description of the great art critic and historian John Ruskin? Who would dare to say so? And yet Ruskin resigned from Oxford University in 1885 when that august institution decided to allow animal experimentation. "The best I could do was wholly at the service of Oxford," he writes. "I meant to die in my harness there, and my resignation was placed in the Vice-Chancellor's hands on the Monday following the vote endowing vivisection in the University, *solely in consequence of that vote"* (italics added, letter to the *Pall Gazette,* 24 April 1885).

Are Robert Browning and C.S. Lewis lacking in intelligence? Who could suppose so? Yet Browning's disgust for vivisection explodes on the page. "I despise and abhor the pleas made on behalf of that infamous practice, vivisection!" he declares in one of his letters. And Lewis is no less stern in his opposition, mixing it with black humor:

> Vivisection can only be defended by showing it to be right that one species should suffer in order that another species be happier...If we cut up beasts simply because they cannot prevent us and because we are backing our own side in the struggle for existence, it is only logical to cut up imbeciles, criminals, enemies, or capitalists for the same reasons.

The Problem of Pain

Lewis, of course, is not himself endorsing the cutting up of imbeciles, criminals, and the like. He is merely pointing out where the philosophy that might makes right, taken to its logical conclusion, leads us. And that is a philosophy he himself clearly does not embrace.

Neither does the great German composer, Richard Wagner. "Human dignity begins to assert itself," he writes, "only at that point where man is distinguishable from the beast by pity for it" (*The Regeneration of Mankind*). More specifically, the thought of animals suffering in the name of science "penetrates with horror and dismay into my soul," Wagner writes, adding that "in the sympathy evoked I recognize the strongest impulse of my moral being, and also the probable source of all my art. The total abolition of the horror we fight against (that is, vivisection) must be our real aim... If experiments on animals were abandoned on grounds of compassion, mankind would make a fundamental advance." (From a letter to Ernst von Weber, 19 October 1879).

George Bernard Shaw is one of the most famous of this century's anti-vivisectionists. "You do not settle whether an experiment is justified," Shaw writes in his Preface to *Doctor's Dilemma,*

> by merely showing that it is of some use. The distinction is not between useful and useless experiments, but between barbarous and civilized behavior. Vivisection is a social evil because if it advances human knowledge, it does so at the expense of human character.

More pithily, he writes:

> ...If you cannot attain to knowledge without torturing a dog, you must do without the knowledge.

> *Ibid.*

And lest it seem that vivisection's only celebrated critics are from the other side of the Atlantic, let us listen to the voice of one Samuel Clemens, alias Mark Twain. Here is the spirit of the man:

> Loyalty to petrified opinion never broke a chain or freed a human soul.
>
>> Inscription beneath his bust
>> in the Hall of Fame.

That is the philosophy of someone not averse to marching to a different drummer. Which is how Twain marched in the case of animal experimentation.

Twain had great respect for the so-called "lower animals":

> In studying the traits and dispositions of the so-called lower animals, and contrasting them with man's, I find the result humiliating to me.
> Man is the only animal that blushes, or needs to.

> From *Following the Equator.*

Twain did not write, but he would agree with, the observation that "the more I learn about mankind, the more I like dogs." Twain however, did write that "Heaven is by favor; if it were by merit your dog would go in and you would stay out" (*What is Man?*). And on the particular question of vivisection, we find the following:

> I believe I am not interested to know whether vivisection produces results that are profitable to the human race or doesn't. To know that the results are profitable to the race would not remove my hostility to it. THE PAIN WHICH IT INFLICTS UPON UNCONSENTING ANIMALS is the basis of my enmity toward it, and it is to me sufficient justification of the enmity without looking further.

> *Ibid.*

Twain is joined in his principled opposition to vivisection by famous Americans from other quarters. By Luther Burbank, for example:

> If, as we know, the creatures with fur, feathers, or
> fins are our brothers in a lower stage of develop-
> ment, then their very weakness and inability to
> protest demands that man should refrain from
> torturing them for the mere possibility of obtaining
> some knowledge he believes may be to his own
> interests.

> Letter to Mrs. C.P. Farrell, 2 October 1909.

So let us be aware of the great men and women who have
been a part of the demand to end the abuse of animals in
science — *all* of it. Let us be sure to share this knowledge
with the public. And let us work against the triumph of the
view that all sane, informed, intelligent humanitarians
must approve of at least *some* research on animals. That *is*
a petrified opinion, undeserving of anyone's loyalty — a
loyalty that will never break the chains keeping animals
in the laboratories of the world.

In the case of eating animals some of our forebears
have used harsh, vivid words to describe both what people
eat when they consume animals and what values we find
in those people who place disproportionate importance on
food. "Disguise it though you will," Porphyry writes (in
On Abstinence from Animal Food), "what you are eating
after all is a corpse" — an unsettling but not on that
account an inaccurate assessment of the situation. For his
part, the famous French advocate of human rights, Jean
Jacques Rousseau, subjects the gourmet to rigorous
consideration:

> I have sometimes examined those people who
> attach more importance to good living, who
> thought, upon their first awakening, of what they
> should eat during the day, and described dinner
> with more exactitude than Polybius (the Greek
> historian) would use in describing a battle...
> Gluttony is the vice of souls that have no solidity.

The soul of the gourmand is in his palate. He is brought into the world but to devour. In his stupid incapacity, he is at home only at his table. His powers of judgment are limited to his dishes.

Emile.

These are sentiments such noteworthy vegetarians as Oliver Goldsmith and Ovid would endorse. And so, too, would Leonardo da Vinci, who writes:

I have from an early age abjured the use of meat, and the time will come when men such as I will look upon the murder of animals as they now look upon the murder of men.

From da Vinci's *Notes.*

Or consider these lines from the great English poet (and vegetarian) Percy Bysshe Shelley:

Never again may blood of bird or beast stain
With its venomous stream a human feast
To the pure skies in accusation screaming.

Revolt of Islam.

And Pythagoras:

Alas, what wickedness to swallow flesh into our own flesh, to fatten our greedy bodies by cramming in other bodies, to have one living creature fed by the death of another!

Depicted in Ovid: *The Metamorphosis,*
translated by Mary M. Innes.

And Plutarch:

But for the sake of some little mouthful of flesh we deprive a soul of the sun and light, and of the proportion of life and time it had been born into the world to enjoy.

Moralia.

And Seneca:

> We shall recover our sound reason only if we shall
> separate ourselves from the herd — the very fact of
> the approbation of the multitude is a proof of the
> unsoundness of the opinion or practice. Let us ask
> what is best, not what is customary. Let us love
> temperance — let us be just — let us refrain from
> bloodshed. None is so near the gods as he who
> shows kindness.
>
> *Epistolia,* cviii

And not only "secular humanists," those dreaded
devils, have spoken for the animals and against their
ruthless exploitation for food. "We have," writes the
Anglican cleric Dean Inge,

> enslaved the rest of the animal creation, and have
> treated our distant cousins in fur and features so
> badly that beyond doubt, if they were to formulate
> a religion, they would depict the Devil in human
> form.
>
> *Outspoken Essays.*

Perhaps nowhere is that form more obvious than in the
case of factory farming. And so we are not surprised to
find Thomas Merton writing the following:

> Since factory farming exerts a violent and unnat-
> ural force upon the living organisms of animals
> and birds in order to increase production and
> profits; since it involves callous and cruel exploita-
> tion of life, with implicit contempt for nature, I
> must join in the protest being uttered against it. It
> does not seem that these methods have any really
> justifiable purpose, except to increase the quantity
> of production at the expense of quality — if that
> may be called a justifiable purpose.
>
> *Unlived Life.*

When Lincoln says "I don't think much of a man's religion if it makes no difference to how he treats his dog," he gets at part of the truth. Merton's point is that the same is true if one's religious faith makes no difference to how hogs and chickens are treated. Those of us who have taken it upon ourselves to be the voice of the voiceless increasingly will be called upon to put our principles where our mouth is. Difficult though the change is, we are all called upon to move closer and closer to eating compassionately, not just speaking compassionately. Vegetarianism is the path we all must learn to travel. Together. Let us all take both comfort and inspiration from the knowledge of the great and gifted men and women who have blazed the trail before us.

There are, of course, more doors to the Animal Rights Movement than those of thought and culture. We have not been doing a very good job of opening some of them.

—Where are the chronically disadvantaged in our Movement?
—Where are the Blacks, Chicanos, and other minorities?
—Who is forging alliances between animal rights and other movements for social justice?
—Who is joining hands with blue collar men and women?

In all these cases — and more — we need to do better. Much better. And we will. For at the deepest level, as Harriet Beecher Stowe remarked, "It is a matter of taking the side of the weak against the strong, something the best people have always done" (*The Minister's Wooing*).

Something the best people have always done...
The best people...
The Christina Rossetti's of the world, who realize that
...other eyes than ours

> Were made to look on flowers.
>> *To What Purpose This Waste*

The William Wordsworths of the world, who see the advocates of animal rights in these terms:

> ...Birds and beasts,
> And the mute fish that glances in the stream.
> And the harmless reptile coiling in the sun,
> And gorgeous insect hovering in the air,
> The fowl domestic and the household dog
> In his capacious mind, he loved them all:
> Their rights acknowledging he felt them all.
>> *The Excursion.*

That captures well what we all aspire to be: of "capacious mind" as we defend the weak against the strong. But we are more than this. We are *for* life, *for* beauty, *for* health, *for* worker safety, *for* environmental protection, *for* the disadvantaged, *for* the advancement of science, *for* compassion, *for* peace, *for* justice, *for* love—always and everywhere *for the good*. For we are affirmers, not deniers. We are for the best, not just against the worst. To get that message out — to help the public understand what we stand for, not only what we stand against — is among our most urgent demands. The public must feel our strength like the pull of a magnet. We must be seen for what we are:

— people with a shared sense of the moral significance of our lives;
— united by our bonds of love, commitment, and our communal confidence that we are in the right;
— tolerant of diversity within our ranks, intolerant of injustice beyond them;
— people who are fulfilled and self-actualized by serving the needs of those who cannot speak for themselves;
— a growing force that may at times bend but never break.

All this — and more — must be conveyed to the public. Increasingly they must see us not only for what we are but also for what they themselves would like to be. Otherwise they are unlikely to join with us. And when it comes to securing justice for the animals, we (and the animals) need all the help we (and they) can get.

For we *are* the best people, those of us who fight for the weak against the strong. And though it may be true that nice guys finish last, the best emerge victorious.

9

Students' Rights in the Lab

A common theme in my talks on university campuses is that there are at least two victims in standard labs in the life sciences. First, there is the nonhuman animal —the pithed frog, for example, or the dissected cat. Second, there is the human student, the young man or woman who, often without pausing to consider the ethics of what is happening, carries out the dissection or vivisection because it is "required".

Most young people live up to the slogan of youth by *questioning authority*. But not many have done this when the setting has been a lab in the life sciences. In that setting, normally inquisitive, independent young people traditionally have marched obediently to the demands of their instructors. The fact that they could be arrested and prosecuted for doing to animals outside a lab, what they are "required" to do while in one, seems not to have occasioned a moment's thought in the moral space most students normally have occupied.

But things are beginning to change. Everywhere there are increasing signs of a new awareness on the part of a growing number of students. Students throughout the world are beginning to recognize and assert *their* rights in the lab. Fewer developments are more important for the struggle for animal rights. The Animal Rights Movement is a part of, not apart from, the Human Rights Movement, and though some teachers seem to have forgotten this, it is incontrovertibly true that students *are* human beings. Nothing we do to protect the rights of our students can harm the rights of our fellow animals.

My own campus — North Carolina State University — is no exception to the growing trend towards recognizing students' rights in the lab. N.C. State is a land grant institution, steeped in the traditions of a largely rural population. The School of Agriculture and Life Sciences has played a vital role in the state's history. A large part of that role has involved treating nonhuman animals as human resources, and a small but heretofore sacrosanct part of that role has involved the routine expectation that students will dissect or vivisect animals in labs in the life sciences.

This expectation received its first close examination in October of 1984. A Petition was briefly circulated among some faculty at the University and then sent to the Faculty Senate. The Petition called for the creation of policies that would recognize and protect a student's right not to dissect or vivisect an animal, if doing so was contrary to that student's well considered moral beliefs. The Petition also asked that a committee be established to monitor developments in teaching techniques in the life sciences that do not use whole animals; this committee was charged with the additional task of keeping the relevant faculty informed about such developments.

The final vote of the Faculty Senate was ambiguous on the topic of students' rights. The prevailing sentiment was that enough already was being done to recognize and respect students' rights in the lab. Representatives of the School of Agriculture and Life Sciences, as well as others from the School of Veterinary Medicine, were able to convince the majority of the Senate that there was no need to do more than these schools already were doing.

Whether true or not, one salutary result stemming directly from this period was the dissemination, through the minutes of the Faculty Senate, of governing policies concerning students' rights in the lab on my campus. Although these policies do not go as far as I believe they should, they do make a public gesture in the direction of recognizing and protecting students' rights in the lab. These policies now are official on the N.C. State campus.

These policies afford some basic protection for students who have moral objections to dissection or vivisection. These students now have public statements that guarantee them the right to demur in the face of ordinary expectations in the lab, statements that also spell out the steps to be taken in case the lab instructor and the student are unable to agree upon a satisfactory alternative. These policies do not guarantee that the values of the student will always prevail. They do guarantee that these values must be heard and taken into account. As such the policies move the University closer to recognizing the legitimate right of its students conscientiously to object to dissection or vivisection.

It remains to be seen how effective these policies are when put into practice. Interested individuals are keeping watch. Myself, I regard the public expression of these policies as a small but not unimportant development on my campus, an achievement in which all members of the University community, whatever their school or discipline, can take some measure of pride. It is a good, a positive achievement, not (as some would have it) a capitulation to the irrational forces behind animal rights.

The essay that follows is the text of my October 1984 presentation before the Communications Committee of the Faculty Senate. The Petition submitted to the Senate precedes the text, and the report of the Communications Committee follows. The existing policies are not perfect by any means. Hopefully other universities will be able to do us one better. But N.C. State has taken a leadership position on this matter, and one that, in my view at least, has not yet fully exhausted itself.

As for the connection between students' rights and animal rights: Remember the motto, "Animal liberation is human liberation"? In this case the reverse is no less true. The liberation of students in the lab also represents the liberation of those animals who otherwise would have died there. Real progress for us is real progress for them.

Professor Mohan Sawhney, Chairman
Faculty Senate, 2319 Library
North Carolina State University
Campus

Dear Chairman Sawhney:

We are writing to you to inquire about the proper procedure for instituting a campus-wide policy concerning the use of animals in courses with laboratory sections. The population in general increasingly resists the proposition that animals should be dissected or vivisected when the factual knowledge thereby obtained can be secured by other means. The University has a unique opportunity, true to its history, to play a pioneering role in recognizing and protecting our students' right to conscience in this matter.

The following statement of principle, if adopted campus-wide, would help insure that this right is institutionalized.

> North Carolina State University recognizes
> the existence of alternative methods to the dis-

section and/or vivisection of animals for achieving the major objectives of teaching laboratories in the biological sciences. Where alternatives are known to exist they shall be incorporated into existing and future teaching laboratories. North Carolina State University recognizes the right of every student to participate in these alternatives and students shall be apprised of this right at the beginning of every semester by the principal course and/or laboratory instructor(s). No student shall be penalized for exercising this right.

North Carolina State University shall establish a standing committee to oversee the use of animals in teaching laboratories similar to those committees overseeing the use of human subjects. The expressed purpose of such a committee shall be (1) to protect the rights of students who prefer to participate in alternative laboratories, (2) to insure that where alternative means of satisfying the academic expectation associated with laboratory dissection and/or vivisection of animals are known and utilized at other universities that they are made available to students at North Carolina State, and (3) promote the development of new methods for achieving educational goals in the biological sciences that do not involve the dissection and/or vivisection of animals.

Would you please refer this inquiry to the appropriate university committees, departments, or offices. We shall look forward to receiving a reply at your earliest convenience.

The letter reproduced above was signed by more than one hundred members of the faculty at North Carolina State University.

The precipitating cause of the Petition currently under review by your Committee was a request for help from a student at North Carolina State University who, for reasons of conscience, was opposed to dissecting and vivisecting animals but who, for reasons of education, aspired to pursue a course of study in the life sciences. Inquiries made on this student's behalf revealed the absence on the campus of any policy that would recognize and protect this student's moral convictions in a laboratory setting. This seemed to me then, as it seems to me now, to be an unsatisfactory state of affairs. That, with a modest effort and in little time, not a few of my faculty colleagues were moved to sign the petition under review, shows, I believe, that my hope that we might do better as a University is not unique. Or worse.

This student was not the first student on our campus to ask for assistance in this regard. Nor will this student be the last. My own experience indicates that there is a growing tendency on the part of students to object, on principle, to dissecting and vivisecting animals, and to seek alternative means of fulfilling the legitimate academic requirement of courses which normally require the use of animals. How large a percentage of students in the future will step forward to express their principled opposition, I am unable to say. As Andrew W. Rowan, Assistant Dean for New Programs of Tufts University School of Veterinary Medicine, observes, openly to object to what others regard as a standard component of education in the life sciences "takes a great deal of courage in the absence of explicit leads from lecturers" (*Of Mice, Models, and Men,* p. 102). For this reason, as Rowan goes on to indicate, there must be a much larger number of students who hold principles that conflict with dissection and vivisection than the number who, in the absence of "explicit leads from lecturers," have the courage to voice their objections.

Of course, numbers by themselves prove nothing. Neither those who favor the status quo nor those who seek change should be swayed by a student body count. But while the numbers are incapable of proving one side right, the other wrong, we should, I believe, be aware both that the number of students who experience a serious moral conflict between their principles and the standard require-ments of laboratories in the life sciences is growing and that the actual size of this student population is not accurately gauged by totalling the number who openly demur in the face of existing expectations.

What *can* we do to accommodate the exercise by these students of their moral principles? What *should* we do? These are not easy questions by any means. Fundamental values, including beliefs about the rights of students and the academic freedom of our faculty, must be considered fairly and, if possible, delicately balanced. This is not the occasion for wild accusations, nor for hasty decisions, and I must express, because it is well deserved, my sincere respect for the evident fairness and thoroughness charac-terizing this Committee's study of the issues to this point in time.

To the best of my knowledge, no American university has to date seriously attempted to perform the delicate balancing act you are called upon to consider; certainly no university currently recognizes and protects a student's right to object, on principle and without penalty, to dissecting and vivisecting an animal. If we were to do so here at North Carolina State, within the provisions of the Petition before you, we would be the first, and, in being the first, we would — or so I believe — serve as a model for all those other colleges and universities that will follow. For there is no doubt in my mind that this right soon will be recognized, if not here, then elsewhere, and if not as the result of a cooperative endeavor of the sort in which we are presently taking part, then as a result of other procedures.

But why here? Why should North Carolina State University, especially given its historic commitment to the life sciences and its growing commitment to high technology — why should NCSU be the first to institute policies like those set forth in the Petition? My reply is that it is *precisely because* of these commitments, when coupled with the great traditions associated with our shared educational ideals, that *we* should take a position of visible leadership on this matter. For there is nothing — I repeat, nothing — anti-scientific in the Petition. Science is neither condemned, nor are its practitioners maligned. There is no call to replace scientific inquiry or the dissemination of scientific knowledge with magic or mystical incantations. What is called for are (1) a policy that allows students to be free to elect to acquire scientific knowledge by using alternative means, when such means exist, and (2) a conscientious commitment on the part of our University to seek and disseminate knowledge about such alternatives. The Petition does not rest on a student's (supposed) right to do bad science or to do no science at all; it rests on our recognition of the student's right to acquire scientific knowledge, when this is possible, in ways that differ from traditional laboratory practices. Along with an increase in the student's freedom, there is a corresponding increase in student responsibility. Students who exercise this freedom will not get something for nothing; they quite obviously will be required to meet alternative academic expectations, expectations which, like any others, they may satisfy well or poorly. In the case of those students whose moral principles do not conflict with dissection and vivisection, moreover, there is nothing in the Petition's provisions that would deny them the opportunity to dissect or vivisect an animal. By expanding the range of options available to all students, we are not diminishing the range available to any. No student will be required to do what he or she finds morally wrong. On the contrary, it is precisely to avoid the weight of such conflicts that the Petition has been drawn up in the first place.

Perhaps it will be objected that we would expand the range of student choice but only at the price of limiting the legitimate exercise of academic freedom on the part of instructors. Both this Committee and the full Senate will be obliged to give this argument very careful consideration. I am not an opponent of academic freedom. Who in academic life can be? What we must be mindful of, however, when we voice our shared conviction of its great value, is that we not ask it to carry more moral weight than it should. Its value is not absolute, not even in the sciences where, in recent years, for example, we have come to recognize and enforce fundamentally important restrictions on its exercise in cases where human subjects are used.

The true test case for us in the present context is this: Suppose a student could learn the same scientific information by not dissecting or vivisecting an animal as that student could learn by doing so. And suppose that the student has sincere moral objection to doing the dissection or vivisection. Is it then a violation of the right to academic freedom to insure that this student, without being punished, be permitted to seek that knowledge without doing the dissection or vivisection? That, as I say, is the test case. For myself, I do not see how this is an infringement on the instructor's academic freedom. For myself, the instructor's duty to respect the ethical sensitivity of students, *when the relevant knowledge can be obtained in ways that respect that sensitivity,* places a morally justified restraint on the instructor's academic freedom. Those who judge this test case differently must believe it is morally permissible for instructors to *require* that students perform tasks which they (that is, the students) believe are morally abhorrent, even when the knowledge sought can be obtained in ways that do not conflict with the students' moral principles. I do not recognize this as a legitimate exercise of academic freedom, and I can only hope that those who take pride in this University and its traditions will agree. The duties we have as teachers to our students limit the scope of our academic freedom, in this as in other morally comparable cases.

There may be those who will say that there are no alternatives to dissection and vivisection; possibly even some will say that no alternatives can be found. These are points that must be addressed in your deliberations. Some aspects of the questions require more expertise than I would presume to possess. I cannot help voicing my personal opinions, however, if or as they directly relate to the issues before us. Even at this date there are computer programs that can be and are being used in laboratories in the life sciences. The development and utilization of such programs and computer-related teaching methodologies are growing fields, fully within the range of respectable science. In this connection, permit me, first, to mention the simulations developed by Dr. James R. Walker, and in use at Integrated Functional Laboratory, University of Texas Medical Branch. And permit me also to mention the work being done in this area by Dr. L. Tucker, School of Medicine, University of Colorado; Dr. E. Glaser, School of Medicine, University of Maryland; Dr. H. Feldman, Harvard University School of Public Health; Dr. J. Randall, School of Medicine, Indiana University; and Dr. T. Coleman, Department of Physiology, University of Mississippi. Much of this work, to a lay person like myself, is esoteric; I am not here arguing my ability to understand all the intricacies of the research these scholars are doing. I wish only to make the far more modest point that such research *is being done*. The search for, and classroom utilization of, biomedical alternatives is at the cutting edge of contemporary science.

That such research is being done is confirmed additionally by the existence of the Johns Hopkins Center for Alternatives to Animal Testing, and by the National Biomedical Simulation Resource Center at Duke University. The importance of this research and its implementation is increasingly being viewed as in the public interest, as witness the recent National Institutes of Health Symposium of Mathematical Models and Computers in Biomedical Applications and the steadily increasing federal funds being made available for research in alternatives. Permit me, finally, to quote from Neil Wolff, DVM, writing in regard to the use of a mechanical Resuci-dog by Dr. Charles Short, Chief of Anesthesiology at the Cornell Veterinary College. "This innovation," Dr. Wolff writes, "has two far reaching effects. Number one — it immediately gives a viable alternative to the use, abuse, and consequential death of live animals; it allows veterinary students and others to continually practice and refine their CPR techniques without (ironically) killing an animal they are rehearsing life saving techniques on. The dog doll is very realistic in that blinking lights and a simulated pulse monitor the effectiveness of a student's efforts to sustain and stimulate a dog's respiratory and circulatory systems. In the near future other features will be added to the model, such as an attached EKG monitor and hopefully a computer system that will be able to simulate variations of real life cardiac and pulmonary emergencies. Models of other animals can also be developed.

"The second effect of this synthetic dog is that it opens up the gates for other possibilities where models can effectively (and often better) be used in teaching." I trust that, if someone were to object to the Petition on the grounds that no alternatives to dissection or vivisection exist, none can be found, and none are being used — I trust that the considerations I have mentioned will be taken into account. For my own part, I believe that the available evidence overwhelmingly supports two of the propositions on which I am most anxious to insist — first, that research into alternatives is fully within the range of respectable science, and, second, that there is no reason why North Carolina State University, given its increasing commitment to exploring the uses of high technology, cannot play a leading role in, for example, developing sophisticated computer models in laboratories in the life sciences. For we have on our campus a rich and rare opportunity to show that advancements in science can blend with advancements in our recognition of the ethical sensitivities of our students, to show that our methods of instruction are progressive, not static, and to show that we are able to respond positively to new challenges without animosity or anger.

It is, I believe, not irrelevant to ask ourselves how students respond when given the opportunity to do laboratory studies using non-animal alternatives. Dr. Roland M. Nardone, Director of the Center for Advanced Training in Cell and Molecular Biology at Catholic University, has for the past few summers offered a course in alternative techniques; 75 students from all across the United States took part this past summer. Some came because they had strong moral opposition to dissection and vivisection; others did not share these beliefs. As representative of the positive responses students gave, upon completion of the course, I offer the following:

> Dr. Nardone provided me with invaluable insight into the objectives. . . of alternative methods to animal research. Ms. Rene Filipowski, course coordinator, assisted me in applying these alternative methods to the lab through proper lab protocol and "hands-on" experience. My goal is to attend medical school

and involve myself in bio-medical research. It is unquestionable that your summer program has, and will influence my present and future research. Please continue sponsorship of this program so that others may benefit.

The course ... was the highlight of my college career to date. Dr. Nardone and his staff presented an incredibly enlightening and practical course in laboratory techniques and scientific experiment philosophy which encouraged me to investigate my responsibilities as a future bio-medical professional. The laboratory experience ... was outstanding and at a standard that I will not likely encounter again at college...

Dr. James R. Walker, mentioned earlier, is on record as saying that "student acceptance (of his computer simulations) has been very favorable."

Having said all that has been said in the preceding, I am conscious that worries over academic freedom are likely to linger in the minds of some. Faculty in philosophy, it might be said, should not be required, as a matter of university policy, to make alternatives available to students every time students experience a moral conflict in satisfying an assignment. Why, then, should the case of faculty in the life sciences be any different? If we respect academic freedom in the one case, do we not abridge it in the other?

For the reasons offered in the above, I myself believe not. I believe there are important differences between the two cases, differences which include the following:

— There is no evidence that students experience a moral conflict when they are asked to satisfy philosophy assignments; there is evidence that an increasing number do when they are required to dissect or vivisect an animal.

— There is no evidence that one can teach the history of the major philosophers of ancient Greece, for example, by finding and using alternatives to Plato and Aristotle; there is increasing evidence that one can learn a good deal in laboratories in the life sciences without requiring students to dissect or vivisect animals.

— There is no evidence that the public has a growing interest, expressed by the allocation of its scarce financial resources, in finding alternatives to the use of Plato's *Republic* and Aristotle's *Metaphysics* in courses in ancient Greek philosophy; there is increasing evidence that the public has a vital interest in the development and use of alternatives to the use of whole animals in laboratories in the life sciences.

— There is no evidence that any student on this campus is unable to pursue a course of studies in philosophy because that student experiences moral conflict between personal values and class requirements; there is evidence that this is true in the case of courses in the life sciences.

The questions this Committee and the Faculty Senate must decide are whether these differences, together with the other considerations offered above, call for the type of institutional response set forth in the Petition, and whether its provisions can be implemented in ways that protect student rights without violating the principles of academic freedom. I have tried to indicate, within the scope of opportunity provided to me, why I think the Petition's provisions should be adopted. I thank you for the opportunity of doing so.

Just two final points. As faculty we share many ideals over and above that of academic freedom. Among those ideals, I assume, are our hopes that our students will increase, not decrease, their capacity for autonomous action as a result of their association with us. All of us involved in higher education must hope that we contribute something to the moral strength of our graduates, helping them to think and act in ways that respect the rights of others while not fearing to assert their own rights when the occasion requires.

As educators our on-going challenge is to seek new, as we protect old, ways that create and sustain an educational environment that fosters the realization of these ideals. History tells us that seeking the new often is much harder than protecting the old. History has brought us to this point of seeking something new, something that will protect, not punish, a student's sense of right and wrong, on the matter before us, and will do so without compromising the canons of science or the dissemination of scientific knowledge. We have a unique opportunity on this campus to respond affirmatively and innovatively. If I may presume to speak for all those who signed the Petition permit me to say, I hope we will make the most of it.

Lastly I have throughout my Presentation addressed the issues under review only as they relate to students' rights and academic freedom. Nothing that I have said has invoked or presupposed the validity of animal rights. I am at present uncertain whether the charge to, and the by-laws of, the Faculty Senate would empower it to consider the merits of proposed university policies based on that idea. But since the Petition does not broach that topic, I have not done so either on this occasion.

POLICIES FOR STUDENTS IN THE LAB
NORTH CAROLINA STATE UNIVERSITY

1. NCSU SALS and SVM committees, operating policies, principles and procedures presently function to oversee and to protect animals in teaching labs, and the Communications Committee encourages the schools to continue to seek outside input in the updating of all related procedures.

2. Teaching techniques other than animal use are presently being utilized whenever possible within SALS and SVM. Additional progressive teaching methods will be periodically reviewed and disseminated and appropriate instructors will be encouraged to consider these alternative techniques.

3. If an undergraduate student in SALS objects to participating in vivisection or dissection lab techniques he or she has several options:(a) That student may select courses from the 21 hours of biological sciences which do not require animal use. (b) He or she may request permission to observe the animal use procedure or be allowed to participate in an alternative procedure. (c) If options (a) and (b) do not satisfy the student, he or she may carry the objection through the normal avenue to the appropriate SALS department head and then to the SALS dean. (d) The student may choose to carry the objection to his or her own departmental advisor, department head and dean.

10

The Promise and Challenge of Religion

With a few notable exceptions, members of the religious community have not played an active role in the struggle for animal rights. St. Francis, yes, and Maimonides. Andrew Linzey in our lifetime, and C.S. Lewis in that of our parents. But neglect has been the dominant response among the faithful. Animal rights simply has not been on their agenda.

This neglect has led to a good deal of hostility on the part of many animal rights activists. Religious believers have been pictured as the devil incarnate. Because the faithful deny that animals have souls — at least this is the most common argument ridiculed by activists — the faithful must think we may do *anything we wish* to the "brutes". After all, didn't God give us *dominion* over the land and the sea? And doesn't this mean that the world is ours for the taking, nonhuman animals included? Small wonder, then, so this argument concludes, that members of the religious community aren't doing anything to help animals. Their theological and ethical beliefs actually sanction animal abuse. The faithful have helped create the problem; they can't be part of the solution.

Now perhaps there are some religious folks who

endorse this argument. Speaking for myself, however, I have to say — I've never met any. Not a single one. The religious people I've met certainly do *not* think we are free to set fire to cats or torment dogs. True, those of us involved in the struggle for animal rights have other sorts of convictions, convictions that go beyond the more common ones that abhor cruelty. Still, that's no reason to overlook or ignore those values we share with the faithful. We aren't likely to enlist these people in the struggle for animal rights if we persist in misunderstanding them.

And enlist them we must. No movement for social justice will succeed — indeed, none can succeed — without the active participation of the religious community. The history of other rights movements, both those that have met with some success and those that have failed, proves this. The religious community is too powerful a force to be ignored or circumvented. A strictly secular movement can't beat them; some way must be found to enlarge the basis of concern and thereby to join them.

How to enlarge this basis of concern is one of the questions I've been trying to answer during the past few years. That quest started officially in 1984, when I chaired a conference sponsored by the International Association Against Painful Experiments on Animals. The proceedings were published in 1986 under the title *Animal Sacrifices: Religious Perspectives on the Use of Animals in Science*. The book makes for interesting reading. Here's just one example.

Those of us involved in the struggle for animal rights tend to romanticize the religions of the East — Buddhism and Hinduism, for example. If only *these* religions caught on in the West, many of us think, then animals would not be treated so horribly. Judaism and Christianity sanction animal exploitation. These religions don't.

Unfortunately, this is not true. The Buddhist and Hindu scholars who addressed the conference proved beyond any doubt that all religions, not just Judaism and Christianity, contain teachings that can be used (whether validly or not is another question) to justify a good deal of animal exploitation. In fact, of all the religions represented, only the Christian faith was given an interpretation that led to the abolitionist position at the heart of the Animal Rights Movement. Whether Andrew Linzey, the author of this paper, will win the day among his friends in Christian theology remains to be seen. But win or lose, it was both sobering and ironic to find the conference's "radical" ideas supported by Christian texts. Not Buddhist. Not Hindu. Not Confucian. Not any Eastern religion. Instead, the familiar images of Christianity. A Western religion is knocking at our Movement's door.

Increasingly, that door is being opened. The newly formed International Network for Religion and Animals is one sign of this new willingness to take the philosophy of animals rights seriously. The reception greeting "We Are All Noah", a film that documents the sad story of animal abuse, and the courageous responses of rabbis, priests, and ministers, is another sign. Make no mistake about it. There is a very large and growing cross section of the religious community that shares many, if not all, of the beliefs that give the struggle for animal rights its identity. With patience, good will, a willingness to listen and learn, and a shared faith in the ultimate triumph of truth, I am optimist enough to believe that more and more thoughtful Jews and Christians will join the struggle for animal rights. How that is possible, and what the current situation in the religious community is, are the topics discussed in the following essay. My thanks to Doug Moss, editor of *The Animals' Agenda,* for allowing me to republish that essay here.

"While animal rights activists have good intentions,

their crusade is philosophically flawed and obscurantistic — based on ignorance and emotion, not reason and knowledge — and utimately anti-human and even anti-animal." So writes Lloyd Billingsley in the February, 1985, issue of the Christian fundamentalist publication *Eternity,* in one of the first — but certainly not the last —analyses of the animal rights movement in the pages of the religious press.

Religion is invoked again in "Face to Face with Animal Welfare," a new pamphlet written by Parker L. Dozhier for the American Fur Resources Institute: "Our young people are being spoon-fed a religious philosophy which teaches them all the animals have a soul and then point (sic) to what they believe to be a *serious flaw* in the Judeo-Christian ethic for failing to recognize this fact." Dozhier, who also serves as associate editor for the trapping industry organ, *The Trapper and Predator Caller,* goes on to argue that "through a cleverly crafted approach our children, as well as unsuspecting adults, are being methodically exposed to a religious philosophy expertly disguised as simply a movement to protect animals from suffering." The article refers to the animal rights movement as a "truly frightening smouldering fire," a sinister cult bent on imposing a minority view on the blameless (silent?) majority. Where will it all end? "Will the Christian work ethic be next?" asks Dozhier ominously.

Much of this inflammatory rhetoric is familiar. Proponents of business-as-usual in the laboratory have for years spouted variations on the themes of "emotionalism" and "ignorance" when attempting to refute the criticism of animal rights advocates. A recent headline in the journal *Medical News* — "Animal Research War Seen As Science Versus Emotion" — is typical.

But what's new these days is not the substance of the same old shopworn claims and accusations. It's their source. Organized religion has just awakened to the fact that there is a strong and growing movement out there that is demanding equal consideration for animals on the basis of morality. The battle for the public's attention has been joined by a new and formidable force.

So far, much of the writing of those claiming to represent organized religion seems to have been borrowed from the research community and other traditional critics of the animal rights philosophy. And with attention of the sort offered by Billingsley and Dozhier, animal rights activists might find themselves yearning for the good old days of religion's benign neglect of the animal issue. Better to go unnoticed, some will suppose, than to be vilified and misrepresented. (Billingsley, for example, actually maintains that the philosophy of animal rights requires a "dictatorship," and that in my book, *The Case for Animal Rights,* I actually suggest that "farmers who raise animals for food be jailed"!)

Are we not better off, then, letting sleeping dogmatists lie? Such a reaction, understandable though it is, however, is not be be encouraged. There is more to be gained than lost by fostering amicable relations with most of the religious community. Healthy seeds wisely planted may not fall on barren soil.

Some Christian Fundamentalists

The gains may not always be as large as one might hope. Among the faithful there are some who are beyond redemption on the issue of animal rights. Billingsley and the Christian fundamentalists for whom he speaks are a case in point. They interpret the Bible in a literal fashion. The do believe in the "primacy of man" as well as the "mystical dogma" that "man is not an animal, but a being made in the image of God." Thus we humans are *in* the world but not *of* it. Our true home is with God in Heaven, not with the animals on earth.

While on our terrestial journey we, of course, are not to abuse wantonly the earth or its inhabitants. In the particular case of animals we are enjoined to be kind to them and prohibited from being cruel. But that, it seems, is about as far as it goes. Our God-given "primacy" carries with it our "dominion" over the whole of nature. As rulers of the earth we are at liberty to use animals in pursuit of our individual and collective good. That's why God gave us animals in the first place.

How many people accept a view like this? It's not clear that anyone knows, but whatever the number is, it can't be negligible. And neither is the power they can wield — and often do. Because theirs is an experiential and biblically-rooted faith, there is little chance of changing minds by marshalling one or another philosophical argument. Attacks on the speciesism of their beliefs will fall on deaf ears. By itself, however, this is no reason to despair of finding any common ground. Even apparently so unsympathetic a view as this is not entirely lacking in potential for the animal rights movement.

Humans, it is clear, occupy a position of supremacy in the theology of Christian fundamentalism. But this is not something we are entitled to take much pride in. In fact the Bible repeatedly chastises human beings for their signs of pride and vanity, whether they be physical or in some other form. A use of animals such as we find in the Draize test, a toxicity test in which chemicals — including cosmetics — are dropped in the eyes of live, unanesthetized rabbits, would therefore have to give even someone like Billingsley pause. It is inconceivable that the God of love Billingsley worships could turn a deaf ear to the screams of the rabbits as they are blinded in tests of such vanity products as perfume, mascara, talcum powder and hair spray. The God of Christian fundamentalists must either be a true God that sheds tears for the suffering inflicted on helpless creatures — or S/he must be a false, uncompassionate God that wholeheartedly approves of appallingly self-centered human behavior for superficial reasons.

Or consider farm animals driven mad in the scandalously close quarters of factory farms, or made purposely anemic to produce extra-tender flesh — as in the case of veal calves. It is perverse — and truly heretical —to suppose that the biblical deity can look benignly on such farming practices whose only defense is that the husbandry methods used cost less or that the results will be tastier. Money isn't — at least in biblical terms — the measure of what is good — though it is said to be the root of evil — and much worry over the taste and tenderness of food is hardly conducive to spiritual growth. Besides, Billingsley's God isn't a Cartesian that supposes all animals are simply machines. Farm and laboratory animals, for example, have feelings and emotions, experience pleasure and pain, and have desires and social needs. Any farmer knows that, and, moreover, these beliefs about animals are firmly rooted in the Bible. So even if we believe in mankind's "mystical primacy" over the animals, the Bible clearly teaches that some of the things that are done to them are simply sinful in the eyes of God. Could a God that despises a "proud look" be anything but outraged at the sight of a $25,000 mink coat?

Those who aspire to help animals are therefore well-advised to acquire some sense of what fundamentalist Christians believe and to explore how these beliefs can be appealed to in waging specific campaigns (for example, abolition of the Draize and other toxicity tests done by the cosmetics industry). Activists should expect resistance, rancor, and breath-taking naivete. Billingsley, for example, reassures his readers that "every effort is made to avoid unnecessary cruelty to lab animals," offering as proof the fact that "numerous regulatory agencies" are in place to oversee the welfare of lab animals. There is a good deal of two-way education that needs to take place if fundamentalists are ever to be enlisted in the animal rights cause. And why shouldn't they be enlisted? Surely it is a perverse moral logic that would refuse their help in some campaigns (say, the effort against cosmetics testing) because they won't support all animal rights campaigns. When the choice is between having people help some animals or allowing them to help none, the choice is clear. The reason for their giving help is less important than that they give it.

Other Orthodoxies

The opportunities for positive cooperation between religion and animal rights activists are no less real when other theologies are considered. Nowhere was this fact clearer than at the London conference, "Religious Perspectives on the Use of Animals in Science," held in July, 1984, under the auspices of the International Association Against Painful Experiments on Animals (IAAPEA). At the conference, Rabbi David Bleich, the eminent Jewish scholar from Yeshiva University, presented his interpretation of the Jewish view on animal experimentation. His was a masterful speech, delivered without notes, replete with knowledge and rigorous argument. It was not a presentation that went down well with some of the animal rights activists in the audience. They seemed to think that because Bleich did not oppose *all* animal experiments, he must be in favor of all of them. In response to further questions, however, it became very clear that Bleich thought that only a very small fraction of animal experiments could be defended by appeal to orthodox Jewish teachings — only the most basic medical research, and then only if a number of stringent conditions were met. Not the Draize test. Not the Lethal Dose 50 toxicity test (in which chemicals are force-fed to a group of animals until half of them die). Not psychology research. Not compulsory dissection or vivisection in the classroom. Not many of the worst offenses laboratory animals are forced to endure. Despite some initial misunderstanding, Bleich did not draw up a blank check authorizing the unrestricted exploitation of animals in science.

And neither did James Gaffney, Professor of Christian Ethics at Loyola University in New Orleans. Gaffney offered his assessment of the Catholic view. Like Bleich, he could not find much support for the abolitionist position in the traditions of his faith. But again, like Bleich, Gaffney found it difficult to explain why, in many if not all cases, animal use in laboratories should be tolerated by well-informed Catholics.

Both men, while not quite arguing the anti-vivisectionist's position, made it clear that their respective religious traditions would require that *almost all* use of laboratory animals come to a halt. Should those Catholics and Jews for whom these two men speak be excluded from every organized effort to help animals because they will not support *all* such efforts? If the aim of the Animal Rights Movement is to help animals, activists must take their allies where they find them. Will anyone seriously maintain that people with beliefs like Bleich and Gaffney should not be enlisted in the future when activists work to shut down other labs no less evil than the University of Pennsylvania's head injury lab? (This lab was closed in 1985 by federal agencies because of extreme cruelty inflicted on subject baboons.)

The Greater Possibilities

Billingsley is not the voice of the entire Protestant religious community, and neither Bleich nor Gaffney speaks for all Catholics and Jews. There are many divergent opinions on animals based on different interpretations of Holy Scriptures. In the case of Judaism, for example, there is a long tradition of vegetarianism that continues to this very day. And some rabbis (Rabbi Sidney Jacobs is a case in point) are unqualified abolitionists when it comes to the use of animals in science. They base their position on alternative interpretations of Judaism's sacred texts. The same divergence is evident in Protestantism. The Rev. Andrew Linzey, already well known for his book, *Animal Rights: A Christian Assessment,* offered a brilliant examination of the immorality of animal experimentation at the London conference. His abolitionist analysis is a high-water mark in recent theological efforts in the area of animal rights.

What Linzey's and Jacobs's work illustrates is that there is no monolithic structure out there called "organized religion." In particular, not everyone associated with religion accepts the notion that we humans occupy a position of "primacy" that permits us to exploit animals as we see fit. The religious community is no less diverse (and frequently no less divided) than the political community. Given this diversity there will be some occasions when the best animal rights activists can hope for is cooperation on a specific campaign. In other cases, however, the possibilities are much greater. For theologies cannot afford to remain static. Like everything else, they frequently are called upon to respond to changes in the real world, and, in so doing, they themselves sometimes undergo unexpected transformations. The recent flurry of theological work on creation serves to illustrate the point.

The first stirrings occurred sometime in the '60s, when people began to realize that we were in the midst of a colossal environmental crisis. Some critics were quick to lay the major share of responsibility at the door of the Judeo-Christian religious tradition, a tradition that taught (so the critics claimed) that God had given us the world to use however we liked.

What did Jewish and Christian theologians do in the

face of this criticism? They didn't abandon theology, that's for sure. Instead they re-examined the biblical and other roots of their faith in an effort to develop viable alternative accounts of the proper relationship between humans and the rest of God's creation. The by-now familiar interpretations that developed stressed the human role as guardian or steward. The consensus that emerged was that we are called upon to be responsible shepherds of God's good creation; we are to be as concerned and compassionate in our relationshp with it as God is in His/Her relationship with us. Our "primacy" must be understood in terms of our duty to serve *and protect*. It certainly does not imply a license to exploit.

Hence the deeper possibilities for the animal rights movement lie precisely in the basic structure upon which the world's religions were built. It is a morally depraved image of the Good Shepherd that would allow us to blind, shock, burn, drown, suffocate, starve or mutilate our animal brethren — all in the name of science.

This good seed — the idea that animals should receive the benefit of our existing morality — if it is well planted and nurtured in the way Linzey has shown it can be, is only a few season's growth from reaching full maturity. When it does, the ethical affinity between animal rights and a significant body of religious believers will no longer be the controversial proposition it currently is. The promise is there. And it is incumbent upon us to make it bloom.

Taking the Initiative

The choice facing animal rights activists at this point is simple. Either we take steps to encourage religion's involvement on the side of animals, or we allow this process to unfold according to its own inner momentum. If activists are serious about helping animals, there is really no choice at all. It is therefore encouraging to know that all the signs indicate that people in the movement already have begun to take the initiative.

Two organizations, *The International Society for Religion and Animal Rights,* and *The International Network for Religion and Animals,* recently formed to promote awareness of animal problems. In addition, the proceedings of the 1984 London conference have been published by Temple University under the title, *Animal Sacrifices: Religious Perspectives on the Use of Animals in Science.* These papers are not the end-all of serious religious inquiry into animal rights issues. Rather, they are a part of the "begin-all".

Historically, we are witnessing the birth of serious religious involvement in the animal rights movement. Given that more than 70 per cent of the population in the United States believes in some kind of deity, the importance of that involvement to the eventual success of this movement is incalculable.

Organized religion must do better when it comes to animals. Non-involvement is no longer excusable — even in a world fraught with crimes and injustice affecting our own species. The significance of a new concern for animals, emanating from inside, not outside, the community of believers promises to be enormous. The "smouldering fire" mentioned earlier is about to be fanned into a roaring blaze. Religion needs the moral consistency that the animal rights movement offers; the movement needs the organization and new voices religion can provide. The new alliance may turn out to be raucous at times, but terribly powerful at others. Whoever leads, whoever follows, the animals need both.

Animal Rights and the Law

During the course of a recent discussion of animal rights — (it was the usual media format, with some guests advocating animal rights while others protested) — one of the protesters declared that there is a large body of law authorizing animal experimentation. The inference we were all supposed to make was that animal experimentation must therefore be all right. After all, if the law is on its side, how can it be wrong?

This lack of ethical sophistication on the part of the critics of animal rights is not uncommon, and even when it was pointed out to this protestor that an exactly similar argument could be (and was) given to defend such infamous practices as slavery, it wasn't clear that he understood the moral and logical defects of his reasoning. Hopefully, others will. For the law is not the measure of morality, neither what is good, nor what is bad.

What the law measures (at least in part) is the public will. Laws are made by human beings, and human beings can unmake or modify them. Why they are changed, whether they are changed, when they are changed — all these are matters that stand outside the law. As such they can be influenced by factors which themselves stand outside the law. Just ask any member of a political committee. When the public clearly is on the side of a particular piece of legislation, few legislators can or will oppose it.

Most people when they think of "animals and the law" think in terms of the legislative process — the *making* of laws. The Animal Welfare Act, for example. But there is a deeper, more fundamental way in which animals figure in the law. This concerns their *legal standing* (or lack of it). The central question at this level is not whether animals ever figure in legislation (to which the answer is, "Of course!"); the question, rather, is *"How* do they figure?" Are their interests protected because the law recognizes the importance of these interests themselves? Or are their interests protected because the law recognizes the importance of *our* interests (for example, *our* not wanting to see bears baited or seals slaughtered)? How we answer these questions makes all the legal difference in the world. How we answer them determines the legal standing of nonhuman animals.

The law, at least in the United States, generally has been disinclined to protect the interests of animals for the sake of the animals. Instead, animal interests have been protected out of respect for the interests of human beings (so-called pet owners, for example, or people interested in bird watching). Legally, therefore, it has been all but impossible to represent the interests of the animals themselves in a court of law. And that fact, which may seem rather esoteric and other worldly, has made a tremendous practical difference. The very structure of the law, its internal logic, has been and continues to be a barrier against recognizing the *legal* rights of nonhuman animals. How to change that structure, that logic, is perhaps the most fundamental legal challenge facing those of us involved in the struggle for animal rights.

All ways of making this challenge should be tried, of

course, including the one that challenges it head-on. That is what I attempt to do in the essay that follows. My goal is to show that the law needs to grow-up on the central issue of legal standing for animals. As of this writing, the law is nothing more than a reminder of an outmoded, inferior and bigoted logic on this matter, worthy neither of moral nor intellectual respect. That protestor I mentioned earlier is right in thinking that the law is on the side of animal experimentation. He is only mistaken in thinking that this fact speaks well either for animal experimentation or the law. An important chapter in the struggle for animal rights will be fought over the validity of how and why nonhuman animals have (and deserve) legal standing.

The essay that follows serves as the Introduction to Volume 31 of the *Saint Louis University Law Journal.* That particular volume is devoted entirely to legal questions concerning the use of animals in science and is highly recommended. It is a pleasure to acknowledge the permission of the *Journal* to reprint my Introduction here.

Some years ago, after a public lecture, a member of the audience who was by no means an enemy of animals took exception to my speaking of "animal rights." "People are just turned off by talk of 'animal rights'," I was told. "They think it's bizarre. Kooky! Why don't you talk like the rest of us? What's wrong with 'animal welfare'? You won't reach people if they don't listen to you." That sentiment was echoed time and time again, and not only by friends of animals. Some persons in animal research and agriculture pilloried the idea of "animal rights" (they could put sneer quotes around the words by the way they spoke!). They didn't like cruelty to animals, I was told, but they liked animal rights even less. "You'll never catch me talking about the 'rights' of animals!"

Well, a serious thing happened on the way from then to now. People started to listen. Not only to me, of course, but to everyone who spoke out for the rights of animals. Even the people in animal research and agriculture — and in hunting, trapping, and the like — even these people learned the vocabulary of animal rights. Today, wherever I go (and I have no reason to suppose that I am in any way the exception), the air is filled with talk of the rights of animals. Not kindness. Not welfare. Not humaneness. But animal rights.

I do not think we should dismiss this change in vocabulary lightly. Ideas gain power with familiarity. When few could, or would, speak of "animal rights," the idea was weak. Today, when it has become an established token in our everyday speech, it is incalculably stronger. Ironically even the opponents of animal rights have aided in strengthening the idea, by using the words they once found unspeakable. That they deny the rights of animals only makes the irony of their assistance that much sweeter.

The law cannot be immune to the emerging power and familiarity of the idea of animal rights. Law changes. That is the first axiom of any political movement. Law responds to changing patterns in the moral weave of the society under its governance. Not just any change. The change in the moral weave must establish the legitimacy of its place in the cultural pattern. It cannot be whimsical. And the change must demonstrate its staying power, its permanence. It cannot be faddish. Otherwise, changing with every ephemeral thought and every passing fad, the law would rival the confusion of a chameleon on a Scottish tartan. Stability in our legal system is crucial. But the ability to respond to emerging changes in our informed, considered ideas about the scope of justice — that, too, is a virtue in a legal system which is devoutly to be wished.

There can be no doubt that the place of animals in the moral weave of our culture is changing. That the words "animal rights" have become part of our everyday vocabulary is itself a symptom of this change. And so, too, are those activities of animal rights organizations daily reported by the media, activities ranging from protests against the "cropping" of baby seals and the "harvesting" of whales, to exposés on conditions in research laboratories and letter-writing campaigns urging elected officials to support pending legislation. The animal rights movement involves many hands on many oars, each pulling the way each knows best, the movement going forward, not at the command of a single "leader", but because of the cumulative energy and power of all who contribute. Here, surely, is a case where the whole *is* greater than the sum of its parts.

But while all these efforts contribute to the forward motion of the movement, there is one kind of activity more essential than the rest if the law is ever to be changed in ways that display the recognition of, and include provisions that protect, the rights of animals. The kind of activity I have in mind is *intellectual* activity, especially when the intellect is engaged in critically examining those received opinions and institutional customs that stand in the way of recognizing and protecting the rights of animals. Among the changes in the animal rights movement we recently have witnessed, none is more vital to its chances of long-term success, in my opinion, than the contributions intellectuals have made. Protests, rallies, campaigns, coalitions — as important as these are, each comes and goes. But ideas — ideas endure. Ideas are the rudder of the movement. And it will be the soundness of ideas that ultimately will insure the granting of legal philosophers have worked with historically unprecedented diligence to identify and defend a set of principles that would secure a new and permanent place for animals in the moral weave. We do the truth an injustice if we deny that these philosophers disagree on some quite fundamental points. Disagreement is the coin of the realm in philosophy. But we do the animals a greater injustice if we deny that these same philosophers agree on other, no less fundamental, points. It will not be possible here to canvass either all the points of disagreement or agreement. I shall restrict my attention to the one point of agreement that seems to me to bear most directly on changing the jural status of animals.

Moral philosophers traditionally distinguish between direct and indirect duties. By way of illustrating the latter idea first, suppose a vandal breaks your car's windshield. He has, we would agree, done something wrong.But no one would be tempted to say that he has failed to honor duties he owes to your car as such. He has, we would agree, a duty *involving* your car, but no duty *to* the car itself. The duty he has involving the car is a duty he has to you, as the owner of the car, a duty to respect your property. His duty involving your car, in other words, is an indirect duty he owes to you.

Direct duties, by contrast, are duties owed directly to assignable individuals. My duty to keep a promise, for example, is a duty I owe directly to those persons to whom I have made a promise, not an indirect duty I have to some third party. And the same is true of many other duties —e.g., my duty not to deceive, murder, or harm others.

All the philosophers who recently have worked on the moral foundations of our dealings with animals would accept the validity of the distinction between direct and indirect duties. Even more significantly, most of these same philosophers would accept the view that mammalian animals (at least) are themselves owed direct duties.

[There are rationally compelling arguments for viewing mammalian animals as having a complicated psychology, as having a psycho-physical identity over time, and as having an individual welfare. Whether the arguments one might offer in support of these same attributions to other animals are as strong is less clear. Still, there is no reason why we cannot be certain what we should think about mammalian animals because we do not know what to think about others. The moral and jural status of mammalian animals should be clear to us even while we are unclear about, say, frogs and ants. I examine these and related matters at length in my *The Case for Animal Rights* (Berkeley: University of California Press).]

The arguments offered in defense of this view of direct duties vary in some details, but a common theme is this: These animals themselves can be, and often are, directly benefited or harmed in ways that are fundamentally analogous to ways in which human persons can be, and often are, directly benefited and harmed. If a young child is burned or if her kidnappers lock her in a closet, for example, then her concerned parents will be adversely affected. Anxious, distraught, and deeply anguished, the condition of their child will seriously diminish their own well-being. All this, of course, is true. And yet no one will seriously maintain that the harm done to the child *depends* on how her parents react — that the existence of degree of the harm done *to her* is a function of how badly her parents feel. If that were so, then the child herself would not be harmed if her parents happened not to care or know about her condition. No, the child *herself* is directly harmed, independently of whether her parents or anyone else knows or cares about her condition. And she is directly harmed in the straightforward sense that her individual welfare — the experiential quality of her ongoing life — is diminished. Thus we are able to elucidate why our duty not to harm her is a duty we owe directly to her, not an indirect duty owed to someone else (e.g., her parents).

There is no rationally defensible basis for viewing the moral status of mammalian animals any differently. Just as a young child (or an adult human being for that matter) can be, and often is, directly harmed or benefited by what we do, and just as the notions of harm and benefit are here to be understood, respectively, in terms of the negative or positive contributions made to the quality of the experiential life of the individual in question, so must every rational, informed person accept that the same is true of mammalian animals — at least. For these animals clearly are not only alive, they *live* their life in a sense that is fundamentally analogous to the sense in which we live ours: They are the experiencing subjects of a life, a life that fares well or ill for them, as individuals, over time, independently of whether anyone else knows or cares about their condition. In this morally fundamental respect, we humans are, so to speak, on all fours with other mammalian animals. Because, moreover, it is the fact that we humans can be directly harmed or benefited that underlies the intelligibility of the direct duty against harming and in favor of benefiting one another, respectively, the case regarding these animals rationally cannot be judged differently. Some of our duties regarding these animals are duties we owe to them directly. On this point, as I mentioned earlier, there is as large a consensus of informed philosophical opinion as one is ever likely to find on any moral issue. And it is this informed, growing, and increasingly vocal consensus, more than anything else, that is establishing the legitimacy of the new, permanent place of animals in our culture's moral weave. How we treat animals is of direct moral importance because it matters directly to them. That is the message. The moral weave will never be the same.

What may appear to be a minor, almost "verbal"

difference — namely, whether we speak of our duties regarding animals as direct or indirect duties — is in fact fraught with enormous theoretical and practical importance. The theoretical implications for ethical theory are straightforward. No ethical theory can be adequate that classifies all our duties regarding animals as indirect duties. Some not unimportant theories (Kant's theory, for example) fail to pass this test, and so, whatever their other merits, must be superseded. And legal theories — in particular, theories about who or what counts jurally — must be assessed in terms of how adequately they are able to account for the independent moral status of mammalian animals. To the extent that these theories maintain or imply that these animals are owed indirect duties only, to that extent these theories are not rationally defensible. It remains for the rising generation of legal theorists to make this case in the rich detail it deserves and requires.

As for the practical implications of the philosophical consensus mentioned above, none is more important than the changes in the law this consensus requires. There are many painful demonstrations of the existing law's institutional prejudice against animals. Time and time again, without exception, animals are denied the independent jural standing they deserve and are, instead, systematically treated as if they deserve the law's attention or protection *only if some human interest is harmed or benefited* — for example, our interests in property, or our recreational or aesthetic interests. Thus does existing law continue to foster the no longer tenable moral belief that all our duties to animals are indirect duties. In doing so, the law continues to perpetuate a system that is, in this respect, unjust to the core. For the justice of how animals are treated by us must be fixed by how *they* are benefited or harmed, not by whether *we* care about this. Unless or until we rewrite our laws in ways that incorporate this fundamental shift regarding whose interests count jurally, ours or the animals', the law, in this respect, must be an object of our shame, not our pride.

The issues sketched above must contribute to the process of change that is needed if the law is to reflect, rather than deny, our new understanding of the moral status of animals. To challenge the status quo and argue for enlarging our conception of jural standing is a salutary development, one from which all those who labor for the better treatment of animals can draw encouragement. The old adage, "You can't legislate morality," may be true. But we are in deep moral and legal trouble if we can't legislate justice.

12

Civil Disobedience

My debts to Gandhi are great. The influence of his thought and the example of his life helped change my life —and continue to do so even now, as I struggle to become the person I aspire to be. Were he alive today, I would be counted among his followers. Perhaps I am.

My dedication to his ideals began with my decision to become a vegetarian. It has taken me a step further, then another, then another. How fitting, then, to include in this sketchy chronicle of my involvement in the struggle for animal rights a short essay on Gandhi's favorite strategy: civil disobedience.

Many people who read this book will be familiar with the nonviolent occupation of the administrative office on the eighth floor of Building #39 on the campus of the National Institutes of Health. That was back in June of 1985, and what prompted this classic sit-in was the NIH's refusal to stop the funding of the Head Injury Laboratory at the University of Pennsylvania. This is the lab whose notion of "research" has been captured for everyone to see on the film, "Unnecessary Fuss." What one sees there gives both science and humanity a bad name. Even so, NIH had decided to ride out the storm of protest. The lab stayed in business.

I was one of the 101 civil disobedients who took part in the NIH sit-in. We stayed four days. When it was over, none of us had been arrested and the decision had been made to suspend NIH's funding of the Penn lab, pending a further investigation. In time all funds were stopped and the lab closed down. It had taken more than 13 months of serious activism and a decision on the part of more than 100 law-abiding citizens to risk arrest. All for a small victory. All to get *one lab* closed — and even then to lose the monkeys to the scientific bureaucracy. They remain in some lab somewhere, for some purpose or other — probably lost forever.

All that effort, time, money and anxiety: Was it worth it? I don't know if there is any way to prove what the right answer is. I think perhaps the best we can do is to ask the people who participated in this piece of history what they thought and felt as they marched out of Building #39, singing the Anthem of the Animal Rights Movement.

> We speak for the animals,
> Their pain and ours are one.
> We'll fight for the animals,
> Until their rights are won.

We all had tears in our eyes. Tears of relief and pride, of hope and compassion, of love and friendship. We had joined in making a public statement about the rights of animals. We had risked arrest. Each of us had proven our willingness to suffer for those who had no choice in the matter. If there had been a mountain in our way that day, we would have moved it!

Was it worth it? I think the answer is a resounding "Yes!" On that day we showed the world that the Animal Rights Movement *means business*. The battle lines were never more clearly drawn. *Our* civil war was formally declared. In a civil way.

That war must continue. And it will. The struggle for animals' rights has only just begun. And so has the use of our most powerful weapon. Civil disobedience. Gandhi would be proud of us.

But a note of caution: Civil disobedience is a fragile weapon. When used in the wrong setting or by violent people pretending to be nonviolent, its sharp moral edge is dulled and can be broken. I address this and related worries in the interview accompanying my short statement on civil disobedience. The interview originally was published in *The Animals' Voice,* and I am pleased to thank the editors, Rick Sorenson and Laura Moretti, for their permission to republish it here.

On Civil Disobedience

Civil Disobedience is a morally defensible strategy for encouraging social change. Its power has been demonstrated throughout history, even as recently as the peaceful change of government in the Philippines. By violating the law the agents of civil disobedience make a public statement about an existing injustice. By accepting the possibility of punishment, they shoulder the burdens of injustice themselves. In this way, civil disobedients accept a token of the evil imposed on those whose interests they represent.

As a strategy, Civil Disobedience is the last, not the first, choice. Other nonviolent methods for effecting social change — discussions and boycotts, for example — must first be tried. Only after these approaches have met with unresponsiveness should Civil Disobedience be used.

Such approaches have been used repeatedly in an effort to bring about verifiable accountability and increased ethical sensitivity on the part of scientists who use nonhuman animals. But despite these efforts, progress has been negligible.

Many activists, understandably impatient with the pace of change, are ready to commit acts of violence. While sympathizing with their frustration, we all need to recognize that there *are* other steps that can be taken. These are the steps leading to nonviolent civil disobedience. The time has come for every person seriously committed to the struggle for animal rights to consider taking these steps. The moral and political pressure for change must increase, not decrease — but not at the cost of violence.

This escalation of activism would be unnecessary if the appropriate persons within the research community responded appropriately. These are the people who now must decide whether to invite civil disobedience or to avoid it, not only on one occasion, involving a few, but for as long and as often as it takes, involving ever-increasing numbers. For this is a means of expressing moral concern which, once allowed to begin, will not die. And it is also a form of social protest whose ranks will swell, not shrink, over time. History teaches this if it teaches anything.

While speaking at the Schweitzer Center in Berkeley on behalf of animal rights, author/activist Tom Regan granted us an interview in return for a leisurely lunch. We asked him, due to the increasing trend in California toward civil disobedience, what his views were on this matter, as well as on the issue of animal liberation.

Do you support civil disobedience?
I'm a strong supporter of civil disobedience (CD). I engage in it myself. But it has to be chosen wisely. It can't fill the whole movement. I mean, the movement has to be

far more than that, it has to be more diverse than that. Basically, what CD does is gain publicity, it's a publicity ploy.

Do you think the kind of publicity we get from CD does more harm than good? After all, don't most people see us as bleeding hearts and Bambi-lovers, and now as terrorists?

Yes and no. I was one of the 101 people who occupied the eighth floor of Building 39 at the National Institutes of Health. I don't think the media presented us poorly there at all. I think the media presented us as a real triumph. And that was because the CD was *very* well chosen, was *very* well organized, *very* well focused.

I'm a Gandhian. That's how I got into the movement, from Gandhi. Any movement for social justice has to have civil disobedience. Gandhi was a master at this. But it wasn't a buckshot approach to civil obedience. That does nothing.

So when I say I'm an advocate of it, I'm an advocate of it wisely chosen and expertly executed. It's got to be a *winnable* issue. That's what we risk people getting arrested for. If we just go out and protest that something is going on in a particular laboratory and get arrested, we get some publicity but we haven't changed a thing because there is no focus.

Civil disobedience should be that toward which we work in a campaign, but it shouldn't be the thing that fills the campaign. In other words, it should be, again, very Gandhian. What we try to do is cooperate with the opposition, "We don't want to do this, we want to find some way to get what we want without resorting to this," etc. And then — when all else fails — *then* we resort to civil disobedience. It should be the last choice, not the first choice, in a campaign. But we've got to have a campaign. You see, we have to have some strategy, we have to have some vision, some focus. We have to know what we want. Now, if we're going to say, "What I want is all those rats out of that laboratory, I want it shut down." Forget it. That's nothing —

But what about World Day for Laboratory Animals? There's massive civil disobedience across the country on April 24th — isn't that strictly for publicity?

Not completely. On that day, in part, we're telling the world: "Laboratory animals never have a nice day." But, also, I think on April 24th there *should* be national civil disobedience — just for the sake of disobedience, just because it's *the day,* the one day of the year when we say to the research establishment, "We're going to make your life as miserable as we can." That's the one day when *vivisectionists* don't have a nice day.

But the buckshot approach to civil disobedience for the sake of publicity plays into the hands of the media. The public's perception of the movement is the media's perception of the movement. So if we're just out there protesting, protesting, protesting, and a bunch of people get arrested, it may actually look like "those animal radical crazies," and that's what the public sees.

The NIH civil disobedience should be the recipe for how to use CD. And I can't think of any other CD cases like that one that have been really effective on the research establishment and public opinion regarding the animal rights movement.

For civil disobedience to succeed as something other than a publicity ploy, we have to get the sympathy, empathy and moral backing of the public on our side. The people who are watching will finally have to say, "You know, I think these people are right." And that, again, is what King was great at, and Gandhi was especially good at it. Finally, the politicians, the people in power, the public at large believe the protesters are right. *Then* we're talking, *then* we have power.

But first, I think we've got to create a kind of reasoned fear in the opposition. The establishment will say, "If you resort to civil disobedience, I'm in trouble." Otherwise, they couldn't care less. We're a nuisance, we're like a pest. We're not anything politically serious. There's nothing to fear from us.

Sometimes power is just the *threat* of civil disobedience. It's no threat if we haven't got a well-publicized campaign. Once the people working toward social change begin to realize that they can count on CD as a tactic, once they understand that the people in power are losing the confidence of the people who are watching, then all we have to do is say, "Look, I don't want to have this place occupied tomorrow morning," and they'll say, "Oh, well, let's talk then so we can avoid it."

Greenpeace activists have the power, wouldn't you say? There they are between harpoon gun and whale ...

Especially when it's a Russian ship out there, you see. That immediately calls for all the sympathy for these people. When the ordinary John and Jane Doe watch this, who are they for? They're for the people in those boats. It's got to mean something. We've got to choose the image, choosing the vulnerability. Where is the establishment vulnerable? The NIH case was fabulous in this respect. And we'll do it again, we'll do it very effectively. And I want to be there with my nose right up against the glass of the establishment when we do it.

Then what are your views about animal liberationists? Haven't they removed not only animals from laboratories, but also videos and photographs that do more damage than anything an individual

protester could ever accomplish? And they're doing it mostly for the publicity, aren't they?

I think there's a way to avoid animal liberation activities, and that is for the establishment to do what April 24th asks them to do: Allow unannounced access into research facilities by qualified representatives of the animal rights movement, such as MD's, nurses, veterinarians, medical technicians, people who know what goes on in a laboratory. And then, if they'll allow that, it seems like a perfectly reasonable check against collusion on the part of the government and the research establishment. Then people don't have to break into labs to find out what's going on in there. There's a perfectly sensible way out of this. They're not going to give it to us without kicking and screaming, so until they do, as regrettable as it is, I think we have to do it illegally.

But, what I think is essential — it's just like CD again — we have to understand the public and what we're trying to do. With covert illegal activities we're trying to rouse empathy, sympathy and concern of the public for what we're talking about. That means we have to deal with the prejudices of the public, that's the irony of it. So if we go in and show a bunch of frogs in a small aquarium or something the public is not going to turn on this because the public doesn't care a whole lot about frogs. And I'm not saying that I like it when all these frogs are being mistreated, it's just that what we're trying to do is reach the public. So we have to choose very smartly about what it is we reveal and how we reveal it, what animals we choose, where the public is vulnerable. They're going to be responsive about dogs and cats, maybe primates a little bit, but they just don't care much about most laboratory animals.

Of course, some of animal liberation doesn't have anything to do with animal cruelty. It has more to do with taking evidence that destroys the credi-

bility of the research establishment.

Exactly. The thing about the film, *Unnecessary Fuss* that was so good wasn't just that it showed what they were doing to the animals, it was revealing the character and the attitudes of these people who were doing it. It was absolutely damning.

What about liberators who vandalize, destroy research equipment, etc?

I'm against vandalizing for lots of reasons, not the least of which is that it's bad strategy. What happens when you vandalize a lab is that *it* becomes the story. The story is not what was in that lab or what the animals were, it becomes "these vandals went in and stole animals." So it plays right into the hands of the research establishment. When we left NIH, we ran the sweepers, we washed the windows, we cleaned up, we polished. We made it as clean as it could be. All the signs were taken down, no spray paint, none of that stuff. It would just be detrimental. We were what I called Norman Rockwell radicals. We were middle America in a sit-in, and that's very important to appear that way and to be that way.

However, what I think is right strategy and right psychology is for the people who liberate animals to come forth and identify themselves as the people who did it. And this is what is really hard to do and a lot of people are going to turn off on me right there.

But the reason it's right strategically and right psychologically is because what it says is that they are confident enough when they broke in, that what they were going to reveal was going to be so powerful in terms of turning public opinion that the public is going to sympathize with them. When they come forward and say, "We're the ones who did this," now it's real civil disobedience. They've come back and are saying, "Punish us." Here's this devastatingly horrible stuff that the system denies, covers up, and here they are, risking arrest, trial and imprisonment, but that's the price I think those kind of activists have to face.

If they're really going to perform the most important function for the movement, that is, to continue to sustain the story, that's why it's right strategy. As it is now, there's a break in, some stuff comes out, it gets dispersed, it gets forgotten. Now what sustains the story? What sustains the story is someone is getting punished. The story stays alive. It's right strategy. And what it says to the public is, "You cannot trust the government. You cannot trust the researchers. Here we are, up against the system. What the research establishment is doing to animals is so wrong, we're willing to go to jail over it." And the public will be more sympathetic. But I don't know anybody else who believes this.

Any advice for April 24th?

Yes. Because of the media's interest, we have to be mindful of why we are there and what we hope to accomplish. We'll be watched as much as we'll be listened to. Perhaps more so. The last thing animals need is another reason to ignore what's in their best interest. We must be absolutely certain we do not provide one.

Shall we be peaceful, civil, non-violent? Yes. That is the order of the day. But obedient? Not on this occasion. The spirit of April 24th demands that we go that one step further in our activism. We must be ready to violate the law, risk arrest, go to jail — not alone. Together. Throughout the entire nation. For the animals. On that day we join hands across America and disrupt the daily business of vivisection.

Be there.

13

A Summing Up

Nothing has been more important for the growth and vitality of the Animal Rights Movement than *The Animals' Agenda*. This publication describes itself as "the animal rights magazine," and it has been — and continues to be — just that. It's the one place where every seasoned activist must turn to keep abreast of the most recent developments in the struggle for animal rights. But it is also the place I recommend new people begin. When people ask me, "What organizations should I join or support?" I always say, "First subscribe to *Animals' Agenda*. Learn what the groups are doing. Then make up your own mind."

Like everything else associated with our Movement, *Animals' Agenda* has changed. Originally its name was *Agenda,* and old readers like myself still sometimes refer to it by its old name. In the beginning it was a quarterly, printed on nonglossy paper. Now it comes out monthly, is all glossied-up, is turning up on newsstands and in libraries, and has a steadily growing number of subscribers. It is, quite simply, the best act in town.

One feature the magazine has used over the years is an interview with activists about their work and vision. I have had the good fortune to be interviewed twice, most recently in the December 1986 issue. I was in the midst of a hectic swing through New England, giving a series of philosophy lectures. Patrice Greanville, the magazine's Editor-at Large, was no less strung-out. Neither of us had the luxury of spare time to give to a leisurely talk.

The interview that follows is the product of our joint labors under less than optimal conditions. And yet I think that very fact — that we were both ridiculously busy and yet anxious to exchange ideas — helped us get to the core of what we both feel is most important. This interview, better than anything else, gives a sense of where I think I am in my own struggle and where I think our Movement is in its. I thank both Patrice for playing the role of Socrates — he who brings forth the ideas of others by asking the right questions — and everyone else at *Animals' Agenda* for all that they have done, including allowing me to reproduce the interview that follows.

Religion, because of its concern for ethics, would seem to be a natural field to take animal rights, but its response so far has been tepid, non-committal or even hostile. Is that correct?

I don't think it's altogether an accurate assessment. In fact, once the religious community sees what the issues are, once we do our job as representatives of the animals and present a fair depiction of the issues, I find that the religious community responds very strongly and very favorably. I'm not saying, of course, that we're going to see mass veganism sweeping Christianity. But I think they see the relevance of the issues we raise to their faith, and they're challenged to respond. It's a matter of growth, process, change.

I asked you that question because religions, par-

ticularly the Judeo-Christian beliefs, are usually repositories of what we might call a very sturdy anthropocentrism. In fact, the liberal denominations — in a world fraught with so many abuses of humans — now stand out for their "super-humanism," if you want to call it that; while those on the right are proud of their speciesism. On that basis, how do you see an approach to the religious community?

I think the religious community is not homogenous. Not everyone out there has the same views about all the same things. In fact there's as much diversity, probably more diversity in the religious community than in the animal rights community. And anyone involved in the animal rights movement knows how diverse we are and how much disagreement there is. So, yes, we should expect to find people who profess to speak for the faithful accepting and defending practices abhorrent to us. But at the same time, there'll be just as many, and hopefully more, among the religious who will see their faith as wanting the same kinds of changes that the secular wing of the animal rights movement wants. In fact, I don't want to separate 'them' and 'us'. What I say is that we need some sort of solidarity with these people. And the change is going to come from within that community rather than from the outside. Hence, all we can do, as active animal rights supporters, is present the issues to that community. Don't expect that the church is going to respond with one voice. On the contrary, there will be many voices, as my film, *We Are All Noah,* shows.

We should be flexible, then...

My view is that we should never take an uncompromising position. It goes back to finding common ground. When I'm asked, "Are you against all animal research?" I say, "Yes, I am." Then they say, "Well, I can't follow you that far." So I say, "Well, how about cosmetics testing; how about the LD-50 tests?" "Well, no, I'm against that." I say, "OK, let's just work on that." So, the answer is not to have an uncompromising position right up front. We mustn't say, "You have to join me all the way to join me part of the way." Let's raise consciousness incrementally to get people to act on what they see is right and feasible in their immediate experience...

As a professional philosopher, I'm sure you have reflected many times on the intimate linkage that seems to exist between humanity's attainable level of morality and technological prowess. In fact, some thinkers maintain that the intuitive road to morality is secondary or false...and that the only reality in this field is shaped by the extent we understand nature...what is sometimes called the "realm of necessity." Do you think, therefore, that as humanity advances technologically we'll be able to aspire to a much higher morality?

I'm not an opponent of technology. I think technology does increase our range of choices. It does offer us the opportunity to grow spiritually and morally. The question is, how do we direct it? Are we going to develop a technology to further subjugate those whom we already have power over or to liberate them and *us?* The most desirable path, of course, is to find in technology ways of liberating ourselves from this kind of dominant relationship we have with the rest of creation.

As real problems of ecological destruction...over-population, political unrest, nuclear war, terrorism, whatever, keep pressing on humankind, more and more people are beginning to realize that the world needs an entirely new ethic toward nature. Do you have any suggestions, besides those embodied in

your Culture and Animals Foundation, on how to accelerate the process?

The first axiom of activism is that people are busy and when you show up with some new cause, it's very difficult for them to fit it into their agenda. So you have to have a kind of tolerance. It's not like the church, for example, hasn't been doing anything — there's the sanctuary movement, the anti-nuclear movement, the anti-Nicaraguan-intervention movement. There's a lot of stuff that the religious and progressive political communities are doing that a lot of people *aren't* doing, so let's be sure to give credit where credit is due. But how we accelerate the process, I'm not sure. The message I try to get to the people is that it's not an "either/or" proposition; *either* work to bring a sense of the importance of animals into your life *or* do something else (i.e., work against nuclear war, apartheid, or in the sanctuary movement). It's rather an "and/both" proposition. The way we make this idea clear to them is by talking about the details of their life — what sort of shampoo they are using, what toothpaste, what detergent (i.e., are they products of animal suffering, ingredients or testing?) If you're going to tell me you can't fight apartheid *and* change your brand of toothpaste I don't understand that. So our great strength lies in the *concreteness* of our challenge. It's enormously difficult to work against apartheid in a meaningful way as an isolated individual. But we can give someone something explicit and attainable to do — they can be activists with a dollar bill. So one test of how we succeed is how people spend their money — especially in this country. Now, as for this question of how we "accelerate" the process...I'd say, 'Go to the mountain. Don't wait for it to come to you.' Go where they're meeting; don't call a meeting and ask them to come because they're going to be too busy. You go to where they're meeting and get onto their agenda and make the challenge as detailed and concrete as you can.

And make clear to all that they don't have to forego all other activities.

The manner in which we present ourselves to others, the way we couch our arguments, therefore, may be as important as the moral substance contained in our vision...
    Yes, definitely. One of the things that those of us who speak for the animals have to be mindful of is how we appear to the world because if we appear as losers, sulkers and complainers, bitter and so on, there aren't many people who are going to want to be with us. That's the mindset of our society. And so the change we're working on, which is a sign of our own maturity, is to go from our adolescence —a period of rejection and rebellion, denial and negation and so on — to be affirmers rather than deniers, be *for* things rather than *against* things, positive rather than negative. Say 'yes' rather than 'no' all the time. And we want to celebrate the beauty, the dignity, the integrity of the animals, and not just spout a steady diet of complaint. We've got to help the public see that the people who are on the cutting edge of doing the visionary work in the movement are self-actualized people who are making something creative with their lives. For each of us — at one point or another — the great challenge is to recreate who we are, not simply accept who we are in terms of what culture, the environment or genetics have given us. The great challenge is to take what we've been given and to rearrange it and to make something new out of all those things. I think that there are people on the cutting edge of the movement who are the role models of that, who are self-actualizing, creative, talented, gifted, committed and who have given their lives meaning and value by making something of it. Now *those* people are the ones you want to be around.

There have been some thinkers over the centuries who have thought that profound structural changes must occur in society on a very broad general front *before* true specific changes can take root at lower levels. Can any kind of revolution occur in one country and not in the whole world, for example? It seems we have a similar question facing us. Can we hope to have real progress for animals before sweeping structural improvements occur in the fabric of contemporary society?

My view is that within my limited time, talent, energy I don't think I'm going to be able to bring about these large structural changes. So what I have to do is work in the existing structure and try to make whatever progress I can there and leave it to the next generation to try to do more. As mentioned earlier, within our civilization and structure there is an issue of how people spend their money. Are they spending it on cruelty-free products? If so, we're making progress. We need to outline the connection that animal rights issues have with the larger picture. The idea that animal liberation is human liberation is fraught with tremendous meaning because the way out of our own bondage and current predicaments *is not possible without helping the animals.*

You mention the church as a fertile ground for education. But the same can be said for other realms of action, other movements, like feminism, for example. Is it fruitful, in your opinion, to try to form theoretical and practical alliances with movements which, like our own, are engaged in expanding the frontiers of moral and political "enfranchisement"?

Sure, I think that it's both necessary and desirable to forge those kinds of alliances. We're a social movement, a human potential movement. The big job at hand for many of the big and small group leaders is how to get people in the movement. Forging alliances like the ones you mention is one of the ways — blacks, gays, native people, feminists, etc...the peace movement, the radical ecologists, the Green Party. In some ways I think it would be tremendously desirable for some of the leading groups in our movement to meet with the heads of the major organizations struggling for social justice, and try to work out where and how we can forge those alliances. I've talked with people in the Green Party in England and they're very receptive. They want to forge cooperation.

That, of course, doesn't prevent us from appealing also to other constituencies which may not be as clearly organized, and which are apparently being passed over...
Exactly. There are many neglected constituencies that we need to get out there and talk to — the religious community is just one. The artistic community is another — not just show biz — but they're important too. I'm talking about the creative people who often set the tone for an entire cultural period, an entire outlook on life and events. The choreographers, TV-show writers, poets, popular musicians. We have a very narrow definition of activism — it's debating a researcher and that's it. But there is a *cultural activism* that we should begin to cultivate. Also, the changes of receptivity are much greater. Go give a lecture to a bunch of biology majors, and then go give the same lecture to a bunch of art majors. The difference is profound — the art majors are sympathetic to our viewpoint. So why aren't we out there talking to the art majors instead of just the biology majors?

The next constituency I want to reach is the elderly. We've never done *anything* with the elderly, always the young people. And this country is becoming grey at the temples...What do we do with them? They've become like animals in our culture. We put them in homes and wait for them to die. We shelter them, we warehouse them. So if there are people whose lives are going to enable them to empathize with the plight of the animals, it's the elderly who have seen the ephemeral qualities of beauty, and many of whom now feel powerless in regard to the larger society. Yet they have leisure time, they're looking for meaning and growth. We need to try to figure out, not in an exploitative way, how to take our concerns to them so they *enhance* their own lives.

Let's pause for a moment to ask a rather personal question. How did you become an animal rights person?

Two main things — one intellectual, one emotional/experiential. The intellectual thing was that my wife and I were heads of a small group called North Carolinians Against the War, we were in the anti-war movement. At the time, it seemed that the way to make my activism respected was to combine it with scholarship and research, so I did research on non-violent conflict resolution and pacifism. In the course of doing that I naturally read Gandhi. Gandhi simply said to me, 'Look, would you like to limit the amount of violence in the world?' I said, 'Yes'. 'Well, what are you eating?', he asked. Wow, I'd never thought about that — I was as blind as everyone else on that issue. I didn't see the fork as a weapon of violence. I saw the gun as a weapon of violence but not the fork. And so it was Gandhi who lifted the scales off my eyes. That was an important intellectual thing. But experientially, we were away and came back from vacation and our dog had been killed that day, hit by a car. It was an accident, but it plunged the family into tremendous grief. And I came through that realizing the contingencies of one's life. It was like I realized in a flash that there was something about the boundlessness of what I was trying to feel that couldn't be contained by that one dog — it reached out to all dogs, all cats — and of course, all cows and pigs, and all the rest. But it was that experience. Philosophy can lead the mind to water but only emotion can make it drink. Maybe it's a combination of the two things. In my case it was both an intellectual and an experiential/emotional process.

I've seen other people go through similar experiences — the sudden realization of our fellowship with others — it's a very powerful jolt to the heart.

Yes, and again, this is related to the more general thing we're talking about. The animal rights movement is providing an opportunity for people to take control of their lives. This is so vital — not in some flimsy ephemeral way — but in the *details,* and in the larger implications...I keep coming back to this — the *details* of your life — that's what you have control of. You can't easily control nuclear power but you have control of the details of your life. Also, within the peace movement, within the religious community...what I like to hammer away at is that there will be no peace in the world until there's peace in your home. You're not going to change the structure of the world if you're not willing to change your life. Who is kidding whom? And there's no peace in your home so long as you keep consuming products directly related to the suffering of animals.

You were talking about reaching out to students, and new fields of mass education. What sense do you get in your travels around the country about the receptivity of college students? Because they are obviously a crucial constituency. They have a lot of free time for activism.

The next five years are really crucial for the success of the movement, because if we fail to radicalize the college students I think we'll have to sit back and really ask, 'Where are we going with this movement?' I think the young have to be fed up with all this conspicuous consumption. They have to be ready to chuck it. They've got to be ready to go back to some sense of alternative meaning of life other than having a BMW and the latest Sony stereo. This is a great opportunity, then, and what we should be doing in a cooperative manner, not in a competitive way, is to be preparing well-conceived, well-staffed presentations for college campuses.

Is there any possibility in the near future, say, in the next five years, of having university chairs devoted to the subject of a new global ethic, one that stresses the sacred interconnectedness of life? We, of course, see the urgency in this...

Sure. Here's my experience with universities. If somebody puts up the money, they'll do it. If you want to create these chairs and you have the money, there will be universities knocking one another over to get it.

You raise the idea that the animal rights movement is *the* movement for the 21st century. Considering the myriad of problems plaguing humanity today, do you really see a possibility to make animal rights the centerpiece of attention? In other words, why should animal rights be the 21st century's preeminent movement?

We are trying to affirm the notion of the liberation of the person — taking control of our lives, assuming more responsibility for ourselves. You can grow in a positive way, in a life-affirming way, a self-affirming way, and the passage from where you are now to where you can be *must* pass through the problem of how we relate to animals.

My view is that the animal rights thing has tended to be very negative — don't do this, don't do that. I've been doing it myself. I'm for protest, for direct action, for all those things. But, I'm *for* something positive, too. This is part of a larger attempt to bring forth the full-flourishing of the human being, and *that's what we're for,* and to do that we must be against the mechanized, routinized, institutionalized exploitation of animals.

You mentioned once that the process of attaining a mature ethic, a true reverence for life, could be substantially helped by focusing first on our respect for animals. Are you saying that animal rights could be the bridge, the philosophical anchor for this moral breakthrough?

Our movement is one that *begins* with the animals, but it doesn't end with the animals. That's what we've got to begin to see. To have respect for the beauty and dignity and integrity of animals; to regard them as having a life of their own and so on, is the beginning of wisdom. This is not one more big ego trip, one more passing fad. On the contrary, what comes out at the end of this is this sense of who we are.

Are you talking about what the Chinese, the Buddhists, called 'the strength that comes from becoming one with the universe'? The peace of no longer being an isolated fragment of life?

There is this possibility of understanding oneself through empathy with *the other,* and this is very close. But what we wish to emphasize is that there is a sense of fulfillment of human life *that is impossible to achieve without going through the door of respect for animals.*

You have just published a new book, *Animal Sacrifices,* and also done work on a new video tape. Could you give us an idea of what the Culture and Animals Foundation is? What are its main goals?

The main objective of the Foundation is to try to find

those creative, gifted people out there who care about
animals, in order to support their work. We need to realize
how artistic our culture is, how painting, poetry, fiction,
drama, sculpture — all these things speak very powerfully
to us. Ask yourself this: when was the last time you read a
poem that *celebrated* vivisection? The answer, of course,
is "never." When was the last time you read a poem that
celebrates the animals? Well...why aren't we doing something with that? Now, when I do a presentation, I work
poetry into it because poetry is a sort of secular Bible.
People listen differently because language is being puri-
fied — the impact of poetry is tremendous.

**Yes, poetry can always have a tremendous impact.
But in the U.S. poetry itself is not as popular as in
other countries. People don't generally fill great
halls to hear a poet read his latest creations. I'm
afraid that in the U.S. pop music is where it's at.**
    Yes, and that's an important point to keep in mind.
Much of the growth of the movement may happen as a
result of trickling down into popular culture. But I'm also
talking about 'high' culture. Usually we're outside the
theatre protesting people walking in with their fur coats.
We need to be *in* the theatre. The question of animal rights
must be on the stage, in the gallery, in the concert hall.

**What do you say to those people who say nature
doesn't have the sense of compassion that we humans attribute to our moral destiny? Nature — they
claim, is blind; it has created murderous food chains
and many other terrors, and we have no duty to rise
above its inscrutable arrangements...**
    This goes back, I think, to the acceptance of limitation
of human growth, and the problem of human self-actu-
alization and fulfillment. It's what Sartre would call bad
faith, to attribute *my* lack of integrity and self-discipline

to nature. 'It's nature's fault that I'm like this.' It's bad faith. Nature gives us, you might say, the canvas. Your past is the paints, you're the artist — what do you do with what you've got? The bottom line, as I see it, is that a full human life is not possible without respect for animals — so that's the first thing we put on the canvas.

Do you see the 'lion and the lamb' finally lying down together?

Not in my lifetime.

Not even in the 21st century?

Yes (chuckle), maybe in the 21st century. Of course, the symbolism there is probably too strong for what we're prepared for right now.

This book may be